LIFE
MANAGEMENT
SKILLS

LIFE MANAGEMENT SKILLS

Joyce **L. O'C**onnor, **P**h.**D.**
Project Manager
Leon County Schools

Elizabeth **B. G**oldsmith, **P**h.**D.**
Associate Professor
College of Home Economics
Florida State University

Published by

HE13 **SOUTH-WESTERN PUBLISHING CO.**

CINCINNATI   WEST CHICAGO, IL   DALLAS   LIVERMORE, CA

Consulting Editor:

Stephanie Cooney, Ph.D.
Curriculum Specialist for Home Economics
Fairfax County Public Schools
Department of Vocational, Adult and Community Education
Falls Church, Virginia

Copyright © 1987
by
SOUTH-WESTERN PUBLISHING CO.
Cincinnati, Ohio

ISBN: 0-538-32130-X

Library of Congress Catalog Card Number: 86-61565

1 2 3 4 5 6 K 2 1 0 9 8 7

Printed in the United States of America

Introduction

Life Management Skills is a text for young adults. It was written to help you get what you want out of life by helping you become a more effective manager. We chose to write this material because of our concern for the many teenagers who leave school without the necessary skills to make daily decisions to successfully manage their lives.

Not many of us like to plan ahead. You may think that there is no need to plan, and that your life five or ten years from now will be very much like it is today. While it is impossible to know what the future holds, it is almost certain that your life will change dramatically in the next few years. *Life Management Skills* can help you develop a life philosophy that can guide you through future challenges and help you bridge the gap between dependent, interdependent, and independent living.

The word "management" may be new for you. Management is the process of using resources to achieve goals. Management is an art, a skill, and a method for improving the quality of life. When you manage, you plan, organize, evaluate, communicate, and make decisions. Management skills help you meet your needs, acquire your wants, and get where you want to go.

Life management is a system that will help you define your values, goals, and standards so that you can make effective decisions. Life management emphasizes goal-directed behavior. In other words, life management can help you produce purposeful change in your life and in the lives of those around you.

The lessons in *Life Management Skills* will aid you in applying management concepts to real-life situations and decisions. The text is organized into seven interrelated, management-centered units. Each unit combines the objectives of life management with the development of a specific management skill. The lessons which compose each unit are designed to provide a managerial framework as you make decisions that affect your daily life. Each lesson features a concept statement which will help you focus on the specific purpose of the activity. A variety of individualized self-study methods, including decision-making activities, skill-oriented exercises, observations, interviews, essays, surveys and case studies, are used to encourage you to develop your own style of managing. These lessons have been designed to be self-directing and individualized. Therefore, many different responses may be appropriate. Remember, you are developing personal management skills. The lessons will be more valuable if you respond to them in a personal manner.

At the end of the text, a glossary of key words and terms is provided to help you review important concepts.

A Teacher's Manual accompanies this text. It offers ideas for the teacher, such as teaching aids, answers to activity questions, discussion points, suggestions for resource speakers, and references. These supplementary materials have been developed to add depth, breadth, and creative applications of the management principles introduced in the text.

Joyce L. O'Connor
Elizabeth B. Goldsmith

Contents

UNIT 4. FOODS AND NUTRITION: You and Good Eating

UNIT 5. HEALTH AND WELLNESS: Keeping Yourself Fit

UNIT 6. COMMUNICATION: You and Others

UNIT 7.   COMMUNITY: You and a Job

UNIT 1

ENVIRONMENT, SOCIETY, AND YOU

UNIT 1

OBJECTIVES:

This unit provides information that will help you to:

- Describe the relationship between individuals and their environment
- List roles and responsibilities of family members
- Define self-esteem and personality
- Analyze personality development
- Explain factors affecting personal achievement
- Recognize the different levels of basic human needs

What makes me feel good about myself? Why is making up my mind so tough? How do I know if I'm making the right decisions? Are my goals the right ones for me?

To manage your life you must begin with an examination of who you are and of your relationship with the environment. Decisions are not made in a vacuum. You need to consider the feelings and rights of others and the potential impact on the environment. You probably haven't given it much thought, but the roles and responsibilities you assume within your family and as a member of society are intertwined with decision-making.

The lessons in this unit focus on you as an individual: your personality development, your self-esteem, and your achievements. Think positively about yourself and your accomplishments. Life is not something out of reach beyond the horizon; life is what you are living today. Understanding yourself is the first step in managing your life.

LESSON 1-1

YOUR ENVIRONMENT

Young adults make decisions that affect their own lives, as well as the lives of their families, the community, and the world.

Human beings belong to a biological class or **species** known as **Homo sapiens**, which is Latin for "a wise being." Human beings are different from all other species because we are able to think—that is, to make long-range plans by:

- Reasoning
- Setting goals
- Making decisions

All of us live in both natural and man-made environments. **Natural environments** include trees, animals, and water. **Man-made environments** include such things as buildings, machines, newspapers, and tools.

We must consider the preservation of our environment as we make decisions. People and all other living things share the need for a good natural environment.

1. Our ancestors depended upon the natural environment for survival. For example, if their food supply dwindled they would move on to another area where natural resources were still plentiful. Are people today more or less dependent on their natural environment than were our ancestors? Explain your answers.

   _____

   _____

   _____

   _____

2. What distinguishes human beings from all other living things?

   _____

   _____

   _____

   _____

3. In the space below, list ten natural and ten man-made environments in
    your neighborhood.

Natural	Man-Made
1. _____	1. _____
2. _____	2. _____
3. _____	3. _____
4. _____	4. _____
5. _____	5. _____
6. _____	6. _____
7. _____	7. _____
8. _____	8. _____
9. _____	9. _____
10. _____	10. _____

4. We have created social and cultural environments which improve the
    quality of our lives. If you had to choose among music, art, and literature,
    which could you most easily live without? Why?

    _____

    _____

    _____

    _____

    _____

5. Would you describe your community (environmental setting) as:

    _____ urban   _____ rural   _____ suburban   _____ small-town?

6. What are the environmental advantages of your community?

    _____

    _____

    _____

    _____

7. What are the environmental disadvantages of your community?

    _____

    _____

    _____

    _____

LESSON 1-2

SOCIETY AND SOCIAL NEEDS

Everyone has social needs. A **society** is a group of people with common interests and beliefs who help fulfill those needs.

Societies provide safe and secure environments. These environments shape our personalities and viewpoints. Most people feel comfortable in familiar surroundings with people with whom they share common interests.

Each social group sets up rules for belonging. You are accepted as a group member only when you conform to most of the rules, such as being on time or dressing a certain way. Groups fulfill our needs for approval and recognition.

1. Your family is your first social group. How does the family affect the personalities and viewpoints of its members?

    _____

    _____

    _____

2. Which is probably true most of the time: "opposites attract" or "like attracts like"? Explain your answer.

    _____

    _____

    _____

3. To answer the questions below, pick a group, club, or organization in your school which you know something about. (Examples are school service club, band, chorus, drama club, athletic team, vocational student organization, and yearbook staff.) Find out any answers you don't know.

    (a) What is the name of the group? _____

    _____

    (b) What is the purpose of the organization? _____

    _____

    _____

    _____

(c) How often does the club meet? _____
_____

(d) What are the requirements for membership? _____
_____
_____
_____

(e) Are there dues or fees? _____

(f) Does the group have leaders or officers? _____

(g) How are the members of the organization alike? _____
_____
_____
_____

(h) How are the members different from one another? _____
_____
_____
_____

(i) Does the group encourage conformity or individuality? ____
_____

(j) What are the rules of behavior? _____
_____
_____
_____
_____

(k) How does the group encourage achievement by its members? ____
_____
_____

(l) What awards or other forms of recognition does the group have?
_____
_____
_____

(m) How well does the group fulfill its purpose? _____
_____
_____
_____

LESSON 1-3

ROLES AND RESPONSIBILITIES

In today's society, roles and responsibilities are varied
and shared by individuals and families.

Roles are what is expected of you. A role can also be a behavioral standard
or function applied to a certain position; for example, the teacher's role
in society.

Responsibilities are things for which you are answerable or accountable.
Household tasks are responsibilities which family members control and
manage.

1. Who is responsible for the following tasks in your family? Mark with an
    "F" for father, "M" for mother, "B" for brother, "S" for sister, "G" for
    grandparents, and "Me" for yourself. Some tasks may be shared by all
    family members. If this is the case write "All."

    _____ cleans the house   _____ prepares breakfast

    _____ takes care of the yard   _____ pays bills

    _____ empties the trash   _____ does laundry

    _____ washes dishes   _____ plans a budget

    _____ does the grocery shopping   _____ makes beds

    _____ vacuums and dusts   _____ gets up first in the morning

    _____ washes car   _____ locks the house at night

    _____ cares for pets   _____ gardens

    _____ prepares dinner   _____ cleans garage

    _____ makes small repairs   _____ drives children to appointments

    _____ babysits younger children   _____ sweeps the walk/driveway

2. Who has the most household responsibilities in your family?

    _____

3. Who has the fewest household responsibilities in your family?

    _____

4.   What happens when one family member has too many responsibilities?

_____

_____

_____

5.   Conflict often arises when one family member does not accept his or her responsibilities. Suggest three ways this conflict might be resolved.

(a)   _____

_____

_____

(b)   _____

_____

_____

(c)   _____

_____

_____

6.   Employment of women outside the home has become a major factor influencing male and female roles. Today, more than half of all married women work outside the home, and men are performing more household tasks. Project what male and female roles will be like in the year 2000.

_____

_____

_____

_____

_____

_____

_____

7.   What can you do today to prepare yourself to accept your future roles and responsibilities?

_____

_____

_____

_____

_____

_____

_____

LESSON 1-4

PHYSICAL AND EMOTIONAL NEEDS

Needs are the basic physical and emotional essentials which are necessary for survival.

Abraham Maslow, a famous psychologist, developed a system that places human needs in a certain order. According to Maslow, **physiological needs** have first priority and must be at least partially met before a person can fulfill higher needs. All of us share these same needs, but each of us fulfills them in a different way. For example, each of us must eat to survive, but what we eat is a matter of choice. The highest level of need Maslow calls **self-actualization**. To become self-actualized means to fulfill one's potential.

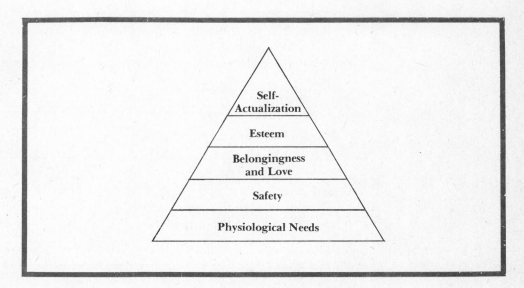

1. Give examples of how you fulfill each basic need in your life:

   (a) Physiological needs (food, clothing, shelter): _____

   _____

   (b) Safety needs (safety from danger): _____

   _____

   (c) Belongingness and love needs (acceptance): _____

   _____

(d) Esteem needs (respect and admiration): _____

_____

(e) Self-actualization needs (development of full potential): _____

_____

2. Self-actualized individuals accept responsibility for their decisions. Describe a situation where you took responsibility for a decision you made.

_____

_____

_____

_____

3. Self-actualized individuals accept both themselves and others. Describe a situation where you accepted yourself.

_____

_____

_____

_____

4. Describe a situation where you accepted another person.

_____

_____

_____

_____

5. Self-actualized individuals seek new and positive experiences. Describe a situation where you tried something new that has helped you grow toward self-actualization.

_____

_____

_____

_____

6. Self-actualized individuals have learned to balance their needs and wants with those of others. Describe a situation where you fulfilled a need or want and at the same time considered those around you.

_____

_____

_____

_____

LESSON 1-5

SELF-ESTEEM

Self-esteem is respect for and acceptance of oneself.

Self-esteem is enhanced when you receive positive responses from others. According to Abraham Maslow, satisfaction with yourself leads to feelings of self-confidence, self-worth, strength, capability, and adequacy. High self-esteem helps a person feel more confident and more in control of his or her life.

1. Describe a person you know who has high self-esteem.

    _____
    _____
    _____
    _____
    _____

2. How has this person's high self-esteem influenced you? Would you like to be more like this person? Why or why not?

    _____
    _____
    _____
    _____
    _____

3. When others treat you badly you develop negative feelings about yourself. Describe a situation in which your self-esteem suffered from poor treatment.

    _____
    _____
    _____
    _____
    _____

4.   What can you do to improve your self-esteem or help others have good feelings about themselves?

_____

_____

_____

_____

_____

_____

_____

5.   Complete the open-ended statements below with the first thoughts that come to mind:

(a)   I get upset when I _____

(b)   I feel all mixed up when I _____

(c)   I get afraid when I _____

(d)   I have a lot of fun when I _____

(e)   I get discouraged when I _____

(f)   I think the most about _____

(g)   I get mad when I see _____

(h)   I feel I could accomplish more if I _____

(i)   I have trouble making up my mind about _____

(j)   I can do most everything but _____

(k)   I really enjoy myself when I _____

(l)   If I had but one wish it would be for _____

(m)   I daydream a lot about _____

(n)   I look my best when I am wearing my _____

(o)   One thing that really bothers me is _____

6.   Review your statements. List at least two situations where you have had positive feelings about yourself.

_____

_____

_____

_____

_____

_____

_____

LESSON 1-6

PERSONALITY DEVELOPMENT

Personality is the sum total of your emotional, social, physical, and mental characteristics.

Each person has a distinct way of thinking and behaving. The word "personality" comes from the Latin word "persona," which means person.

Your family has a major impact on how your personality develops. You develop good feelings about yourself when people treat you with love, kindness, trust, and understanding. You develop bad feelings about yourself when people treat you poorly. These experiences shape your self-image and affect your self-esteem.

Your personality is a combination of how you feel about yourself, how you want to be, and how you act around others.

1. Check three characteristics in the list below which best describe your personality:

    _____ adventuresome _____ friendly _____ quiet

    _____ ambitious _____ generous _____ responsible

    _____ competitive _____ helpful _____ shy

    _____ considerate _____ humble _____ tolerant

    _____ courageous _____ kind _____ tough

    _____ creative _____ outgoing _____ understanding

2. Ask a friend or parent to look over this list. What three characteristics do they think best describe your personality?

    _____

3. Sometimes how you see yourself is different from how others see you.

    Did your choices match those of your friend or parent? _____

    Explain the similarity or difference. _____

    _____

    _____

4. Answer the questions below by circling the face that best illustrates how you feel. Consider not just how you feel today but how you have felt in the past year.

How are things going?

How do you feel about:

(a) Yourself? ....

(b) Your community? ....

(c) Your friends? ....

(d) Your school? ....

(e) Your family? ....

(f) The national government? ....

(g) Television shows? ....

(h) Your social life? ....

(i) The state of the world? ....

(j) How others see you? ....

(k) Where your life is going? ....

Totals: .... _____ _____ _____

5. Which face did you circle the most? _____

What does this say about how you feel things are going?

_____

_____

_____

LESSON 1-7

ACHIEVEMENT

To **achieve** means to accomplish or finish with success.

Each person has a need to achieve. Achievement requires exertion, skill, practice, and perseverance. It also requires independence and a set of well-defined goals.

Studies of adult achievers indicate that they worry less than other people about what others think, and they are willing to take risks. Fear of failure keeps many people from trying to achieve.

1. Even small achievements can raise your self-esteem. Give examples of achievements or successes you have experienced and name the person or persons who encouraged you to achieve:

Type of Achievement	Your Specific Achievement or Success	Person(s) Who Encouraged You
(a) School achievement	_____	_____
(b) Work achievement	_____	_____
(c) Athletic achievement	_____	_____
(d) Artistic or musical achievement	_____	_____
(e) Other achievement	_____	_____

2. Which type of teacher would probably encourage you most to achieve: one who is warm, empathetic, and understanding or one who is cold, aloof, and brilliant? Explain your answer.

_____

_____

_____

_____

_____

15

3.   **(a)**   Describe the last time you felt successful.

_____

_____

_____

_____

_____

   (b)   Who was with you? _____

   (c)   What were you doing? _____

_____

_____

   (d)   Are you planning to build on that previous success? If so, how?

_____

_____

_____

4.   Being afraid some of the time is natural and normal. Have you ever had any of the fears listed below? Check the ones you've experienced.

_____ fear of making a mistake   _____ fear of being criticized

_____ fear of appearing foolish   _____ fear of being alone

_____ fear of being different   _____ fear of voicing an opinion

5.   According to studies, the most common fear is the fear of public speaking. Why do you think this is more common than the fear of snakes, natural disasters, or plane crashes?

_____

_____

_____

_____

6.   Describe a situation in which you encouraged another person to achieve. How did this experience make you feel?

_____

_____

_____

_____

_____

_____

UNIT 2

MANAGEMENT: YOUR GOALS, DECISIONS, AND RESOURCES

UNIT 2

OBJECTIVES:

This unit provides information that will help you to:

■ Interpret the management process

■ Define goals, needs, standards, and resources

■ Analyze values

■ Recognize time as a resource

■ Identify the components of effective decision-making

■ Practice problem-solving

You were born into a complex world that runs at a hectic pace. While the word "management" may mean very little to you now, you will use the principles of management the rest of your life in whatever vocation you choose. Management is the foundation for achieving goals; the processes of planning and decision-making provide the basis for learning, for appraising needs, wants, and resources, and for making educational and occupational choices. Developing decision-making skills can help you keep up with the pace of daily living and at the same time develop a positive self-concept.

Knowledge of the management process does not guarantee that you will get what you want out of life. **Motivation** is a key component: You must want to achieve your goals. The lessons in this unit will help you view management as a framework for coping with the many decisions you make each day. Establishing new goals or prioritizing old ones will help you distinguish between goals that are likely to lead to a satisfying life and those that will lead to disappointment.

LESSON 2-1

THE MANAGEMENT PROCESS

Management is the process of using resources to achieve goals.

Management provides a framework for coping with life events. Management helps us control and influence situations. **Resources** (that is, time, energy, money) are what you use to get what you want. Management is both an art and a method for improving the quality of life.

1. Managers perform many functions. Give an example of a situation in which you:

    (a) Planned ahead _____

    _____

    (b) Made a decision _____

    _____

    (c) Set goals _____

    _____

    (d) Saved time _____

    _____

    (e) Used organizational skills _____

    _____

    (f) Communicated ideas _____

    _____

    (g) Set rules _____

    _____

    (h) Obtained agreement _____

    _____

    (i) Reduced tension or conflict _____

    _____

2.   What management functions are performed by teachers?

_____

_____

3.   What management functions are performed by parents?

_____

_____

4.   Has your method of managing ever been influenced by a lack of resources? Explain your answer.

_____

_____

_____

_____

_____

5.   Why will it be necessary to change the way you manage as you get older?

_____

_____

_____

_____

_____

6.   (a)   Check any of the following management experiences which you have already had:

_____ managed a business or enterprise (paper route, yard work, etc.)

_____ managed a fund-raising event

_____ managed an athletic team or event

_____ managed young children

_____ managed a club or class project

_____ managed money or saved up for something

_____ other (explain) _____

_____

(b)   How have these experiences increased your ability to manage?

_____

_____

_____

_____

_____

_____

LESSON 2-2

GOALS

Goals are what you want to achieve; they help you get what you want out of life.

There are three kinds of goals: short-term, intermediate, and long-term. Earning a high school diploma is a long-term goal many teens share.

- **Short-term goals** can be completed in a few hours or days.
- **Intermediate goals** take between a week to six months to achieve.
- **Long-term goals** take over six months to achieve.

1. Setting realistic individual goals—ones that can be achieved—is very important. In the spaces below write three goals for each category and enter the anticipated date of accomplishment:

Time Frame	Goals	Anticipated Date
(a) Short-term .... (hours, days, up to a week)	_____	_____
	_____	_____
	_____	_____
	_____	_____
(b) Intermediate .... (one week to six months)	_____	_____
	_____	_____
	_____	_____
	_____	_____
(c) Long-term .... (six months or more)	_____	_____
	_____	_____
	_____	_____
	_____	_____

2.   Imagine your life five years from now. Your age will be _____ .
What long-term goal (from Question 1) have you accomplished? Write a
paragraph describing your goal achievement, your life, where you are
living, and with whom you are living.

_____

_____

_____

_____

_____

_____

_____

_____

_____

_____

_____

_____

3.   Describe a typical day in your life five years from now.

_____

_____

_____

_____

_____

_____

_____

4.   What are you doing now to try to make the life you desire happen?

_____

_____

_____

_____

_____

_____

_____

_____

LESSON 2-3

VALUES

Values are principles that guide behavior. The family is
fundamental in value formation.

Values come from many different sources. During the early childhood years
values come from your family. During the teenage years the **peer group**
(friends) gains importance and become a strong influence on your values.

1. Check the values on the list below which are important to you. Add
    other values if you wish:

    _____ independence   _____ thrift

    _____ patriotism   _____ love

    _____ honesty   _____ health

    _____ creativity   _____ responsibility

    _____ courage   _____ freedom

    _____ ambition   _____ service to others

    _____ happiness   _____ forgiveness

    _____ kindness   _____ loyalty

    _____ security   _____

    _____ intelligence   _____

    _____ cheerfulness   _____

2. Review the values you have checked. Select the one which is the most
    important to you. Write a paragraph describing a situation in your life
    in which this value was important.

    _____

    _____

    _____

    _____

    _____

    _____

    _____

3. Explain how your peer group has influenced your values.

    _____

    _____

    _____

    _____

    _____

4. Using the values continuum below, place an "X" marking your position (how you feel most of the time) on the lines. For example, if you never buy brand names then the "X" would be at the left end of the line. There are no right or wrong answers.

ISSUE: BRAND NAME PRODUCTS

I never   I always
buy brand _____ buy brand
names   names

ISSUE: TAKING CHANCES

Safety _____ Risk

ISSUE: TELEVISION

Often   Seldom
Watch TV _____ Watch TV

ISSUE: FRIENDSHIPS

Not   Very
Important _____ Important

ISSUE: HONESTY

Always the   Never the
Best Policy _____ Best Policy

ISSUE: CONVENIENCE FOODS

Always   Never
Use _____ Use

ISSUE: MAKING MONEY

Not   Very
Important _____ Important

ISSUE: WINNING COMPETITIONS

Not   Very
Important _____ Important

LESSON 2-4

STANDARDS

Standards are judgments used to measure progress toward goals. They are what you see as the ideal of performance.

Standards vary considerably from person to person. For example, what you think is "A" work might not be what your teacher thinks is "A" work. What you think is a great job of mowing the lawn might not meet your neighbor's standard of a great job. Reconciling your standards of performance with those of family and employers is a lifelong task.

1. Why are standards necessary? _____
    _____
    _____

2. Who sets the standards at your house? _____
    _____

3. Who sets the standards at school? _____
    _____

4. List some personal standards that you try to maintain.
    _____
    _____
    _____

5. Can an individual's standards be determined from outward appearances?
    Explain your answer. _____
    _____
    _____
    _____
    _____
    _____
    _____

6. Societal standards are reflected in television programming. Write an essay on the values and standards portrayed on current family-oriented television programs.

_____

_____

_____

_____

_____

_____

_____

_____

_____

_____

_____

_____

_____

_____

_____

_____

_____

_____

_____

_____

_____

_____

_____

_____

_____

_____

_____

LESSON 2-5

RESOURCES

Resources are the things you can use to achieve a goal.

Resources can be divided into two categories: human and non-human. **Human resources** are the skills, talents, knowledge, and abilities which you possess. Your ability to read these words is a human resource. Human resources usually increase through use. Food, clothes, and houses are all examples of **material resources**. These resources decrease or become worn through use.

1.   Select and describe a goal which you would like to accomplish within the next week.

_____

_____

2.   Name the resources you plan to use to achieve your goal.

Human Resources	Material Resources
_____	_____
_____	_____
_____	_____
_____	_____

3.   Briefly state how you are going to use your resources to achieve your goal.

_____

_____

_____

_____

_____

_____

4.   (a)   List ten material resources in your home that use electricity or gas.

1. _____   6. _____

2. _____   7. _____

3. _____   8. _____

4. _____   9. _____

5. _____   10. _____

(b)   Draw a line through the three things you could most easily live without.

(c)   Draw a circle around the three things you absolutely would not want to give up.

5.   (a)   Make a list of ten material resources that you own (records, clothing, bedroom furniture, etc.).

1. _____   6. _____

2. _____   7. _____

3. _____   8. _____

4. _____   9. _____

5. _____   10. _____

(b)   Draw a line through the three things you could most easily live without.

(c)   Draw a circle around the three things you absolutely would not want to give up.

6.   What conclusions have you been able to draw from this exercise concerning material resources?

_____

_____

_____

_____

_____

LESSON 2-6

RESOURCEFULNESS

Resourcefulness is your capacity for effectively using the resources you have to cope with daily challenges.

1. Below is a list of human and material resources. Place the letter "H" by the human resources and the letter "M" by the material resources:

    _____ bank   _____ knowing how to diaper a baby

    _____ boat   _____ television

    _____ artistic talent   _____ books

    _____ library   _____ imagination

    _____ water   _____ sewing ability

    _____ cooking ability   _____ computer

    _____ cake mix   _____ sewing machine

    _____ checking account   _____ ability to follow instructions

    _____ swimming ability   _____ writing ability

    _____ knowledge   _____ cheerful personality

2. Often you must possess a human resource in order to use a material resource. Give several examples of this from your own experience.

    _____

    _____

    _____

    _____

    _____

    _____

    _____

    _____

    _____

3.   Review the human resources you have marked. Select the one which is
     most important to you. Write a paragraph describing a situation in your
     life in which this resource was important.

     _____

     _____

     _____

     _____

     _____

     _____

     _____

4.   List three human resources you would like to improve or develop.

     (a)   _____

     (b)   _____

     (c)   _____

5.   List three material resources you would like to have.

     (a)   _____

     (b)   _____

     (c)   _____

6.   Describe how you plan to acquire or develop these human and material
     resources.

     _____

     _____

     _____

     _____

     _____

     _____

     _____

     _____

     _____

     _____

     _____

     _____

     _____

LESSON 2-7

TIME MANAGEMENT

Time management is the conscious control of your time
to fulfill your needs and achieve your goals.

Time is a resource that is equal for everyone. How you choose to spend
your time is based on your values.

   Discretionary time is the free time you have to use any way you want.
Non-discretionary time is time that you cannot regulate yourself. For example,
school hours are non-discretionary because they are established by the school.
In the course of the school day, however, you have some discretionary time
between classes, in the cafeteria, and in study halls when you can make choices
about whom to be with and what to study.

1.   Does discretionary time increase or decrease as you get older? Explain
     your answer. _____

     _____

     _____

2.   What is your favorite day of the week? Why? _____

     _____

     _____

3.   Why do many people say Monday is their least favorite day of the week?

     _____

     _____

4.   **Procrastination,** which means putting things off, is a major time man-
     agement problem for many people. Give an example of a situation in
     which you procrastinated. Explain why you procrastinated and how the
     situation turned out.

     _____

     _____

     _____

     _____

5. To discover your attitudes toward time, check your responses to the following questions:

	Yes	No	Sometimes
(a) Does it annoy you when you are late to class?	_____	_____	_____
(b) Do you look at clocks and watches a lot?	_____	_____	_____
(c) Do you often feel rushed?	_____	_____	_____
(d) Does it bother you to be late to a movie?	_____	_____	_____
(e) Do you hate waiting in long lines?	_____	_____	_____
(f) Do you feel it is important for others to be on time?	_____	_____	_____
(g) Do you often make lists of things to do?	_____	_____	_____
(h) Do you feel there are not enough hours in the day to do all you want to do?	_____	_____	_____
(i) Do you have your own calendar or appointment book?	_____	_____	_____
(j) Would it bother you to wait ten minutes for a ride home after a school or sporting event?	_____	_____	_____
Totals:	_____	_____	_____

8-10 Yes answers indicate that you are very time-conscious.
4-7 Yes answers indicate that you are moderately time-conscious.
0-3 Yes answers indicate that you are not very time-conscious.

6. If, as a society, we changed from a five-day work week to a four-day work week, what do you think most people would do with an extra day of discretionary time?

_____

_____

_____

LESSON 2-8

TIME LOG

A time log is a method of keeping track of how you spend your time.

One of the best ways to get an accurate picture of how you spend your time is to keep a time log for at least two weeks. As a starting point complete the time logs below. List your major activities for a typical school day and for Saturday. In the "reaction" column write how you feel about the way your time is spent.

Time Log: Typical School Day

Time	Activity	Reaction
Morning:		
7:00-8:00	_____	_____
8:00-9:00	_____	_____
9:00-10:00	_____	_____
10:00-11:00	_____	_____
11:00-12:00	_____	_____
Afternoon:		
12:00-1:00	_____	_____
1:00-2:00	_____	_____
2:00-3:00	_____	_____
3:00-4:00	_____	_____
4:00-5:00	_____	_____
5:00-6:00	_____	_____
Evening:		
6:00-7:00	_____	_____
7:00-8:00	_____	_____
8:00-9:00	_____	_____

Time Log: Typical Saturday

Time	Activity	Reaction
Morning:		
7:00-8:00	_____	_____
8:00-9:00	_____	_____
9:00-10:00	_____	_____
10:00-11:00	_____	_____
11:00-12:00	_____	_____
Afternoon:		
12:00-1:00	_____	_____
1:00-2:00	_____	_____
2:00-3:00	_____	_____
3:00-4:00	_____	_____
4:00-5:00	_____	_____
5:00-6:00	_____	_____
Evening:		
6:00-7:00	_____	_____
7:00-8:00	_____	_____
8:00-9:00	_____	_____

1. How is your Saturday schedule different from your school-day schedule?

    _____

    _____

    _____

    _____

    _____

2. How can you use your free time better?

    _____

    _____

    _____

    _____

    _____

    _____

LESSON 2-9

TIME USE EVALUATION

Time evaluation means to determine the value or worth of how you spend your time.

Recording how you spend your time through a time log is the first step in understanding where your time goes. The second step is to evaluate your time use.

1. Look at the reactions section of your time log in Lesson 2-8. Are you using your time as effectively as you could be? _____

2. Another way to evaluate your time use is through the subtraction method of time analysis. Fill in the blanks based on how you spend your time on a typical weekday. Interview your parent or guardian as a means of comparison.

	You	Parent
	24 Hours	*24 Hours*
Number of hours in school	− _____	− _____
Subtotal		
Number of hours at work	− _____	− _____
Subtotal		
Number of hours sleeping	− _____	− _____
Subtotal		
Number of hours in personal care (shower, hair, etc.)	− _____	− _____
Subtotal		
Number of hours for transportation	− _____	− _____
Subtotal		
Number of hours eating	− _____	− _____
Subtotal		
Number of hours doing housework, food preparation, child care and shopping	− _____	− _____
Subtotal		
Number of hours left	_____	_____

(a)   How many hours are left for leisure activities? _____

(b)   How do you feel about how your time is spent during an average day?

_____

_____

(c)   Where do you need to cut down on time spent? _____

_____

(d)   Where do you need to spend more time? _____

_____

3.   Some people think daily about their time use and their progress toward goals. Others do it on payday, on their birthday, or on New Year's Eve. When do you evaluate how you spend your time?

_____

4.   Imagine you are being interviewed by a newspaper reporter on your fiftieth birthday. You are asked to name your five most important achievements. How would you like to be able to answer this question?

1. _____

2. _____

3. _____

4. _____

5. _____

5.   What are the main differences between how you spend your time and how your parents spend their time? _____

_____

_____

_____

_____

LESSON 2-10

DECISION-MAKING

Decision-making is the process of making conscious choices between two or more alternatives to achieve a goal.

In the course of a day, everyone makes hundreds of decisions. When children are young, parents make the big decisions. As a teenager you are responsible for making many of your own decisions. Decision-making involves several steps:

- Identifying the problem that requires action
- Examining goals and considering resources
- Considering all the alternatives
- Choosing one alternative
- Making the decision
- Acting on the decision
- Evaluating the decision

1. Give an example of a decision you made recently.

_____

_____

_____

2. What alternatives did you consider?

_____

_____

_____

_____

3. Which alternative did you choose?

_____

_____

_____

4.   How did you implement (take action on) the decision?

_____

_____

_____

_____

_____

5.   After making the decision, did you evaluate the outcome?

_____

_____

6.   Did you choose the best possible alternative? Explain your answer.

_____

_____

_____

_____

_____

7.   If not, which alternative should you have chosen?

_____

_____

_____

_____

_____

8.   If you were faced with a similar decision in the future, what would you do differently?

_____

_____

_____

_____

_____

_____

_____

_____

LESSON 2-11

DECISION-MAKING CASE STUDY

Decisions are more effective when thinking and reasoning are used in making them.

Lee Wright is a senior at John F. Kennedy High School. She is finding it difficult to decide what to do after graduation. She must decide either to go to college or to get a job as a secretary at a local business.

Lee's father would like for her to go to college while he is still financially able to help with her expenses. Lee's mother feels that it would be a mistake for Lee to get out of the habit of studying and has often commented that once you quit school it is hard to return. Lee, however, wants to have a job, car, and apartment of her own. She feels that her parents have done a lot for her already and that it is now time for her to be independent.

1. What values (principles that guide behavior) is Lee expressing or implying?

   _____

   _____

   _____

   _____

   _____

   _____

   _____

2. What values are Lee's parents expressing or implying?

   _____

   _____

   _____

   _____

   _____

   _____

   _____

3.   What facts are to be considered?

_____

_____

_____

_____

_____

_____

4.   Identify possible alternatives to be considered.

_____

_____

_____

_____

_____

_____

5.   What decision would you make if you were Lee?

_____

_____

_____

_____

_____

_____

6.   What reasons can you give for the decision?

_____

_____

_____

_____

_____

_____

LESSON 2-12

PROBLEM-SOLVING

Problem-solving involves taking action to resolve a question or situation which is uncertain or difficult.

When solving problems you try to anticipate the possible outcomes (results). Problem-solving usually leads to changes in your course of action.

1. Describe a problem you are trying to solve.

   _____

   _____

   _____

   _____

2. Consider possible outcomes of the problem you described in Question 1. List below possible positive and negative outcomes.

Positive Outcomes	Negative Outcomes
_____	_____
_____	_____
_____	_____
_____	_____

3. Examine the facts and feelings involved with the problem in Question 1. Write a statement on how these facts and feelings affect each possible outcome. Consider the situation, circumstances, and people involved in the problem.

   _____

   _____

   _____

   _____

   _____

4. To solve your problem, will you need any personal or material resources? Do you need more information? Are there any value conflicts? How will others be affected by your method of problem-solving and its result? Are you being influenced by others? If so, is it positive or negative influence?

_____

_____

_____

_____

_____

_____

_____

_____

_____

_____

_____

_____

_____

_____

_____

_____

_____

_____

_____

_____

5. List possible alternative solutions to your problem. Ask others for suggestions if necessary.

_____

_____

_____

_____

_____

_____

_____

_____

UNIT 3

PERSONAL FINANCE: YOU AND MONEY

UNIT 3

This unit provides information that will help you to:

- Understand the American economic system
- List consumer rights and responsibilities
- Analyze the use of consumer credit
- Differentiate between informational and emotional advertising
- Define personal financial goals
- Prepare a personal budget, a net worth statement, and banking forms

Many of life's most important decisions are those concerning the management of consumer resources. Since money is necessary for satisfying needs and achieving many goals, it is important to develop skill in money management. Money is the one resource that is related to earning, spending, borrowing, and investing. Money does more for you than buy what you need and want—it influences how you feel about yourself and others. It affects your standard of living and your future career goals. Money, or the lack of it, often is related to your self-esteem and the degree of satisfaction you gain from life.

Personal financial management is a learned skill—one that requires time and practice to develop. Learning to set realistic financial goals and follow a spending plan are the first steps in guiding financial decisions for the present as well as the future. Planning is essential in money management because it forces you to think things through before spending. Too often, people are influenced by emotional advertising to "buy now." The lessons in this unit will help you to understand how to live within your income, realize your financial goals, and protect your consumer rights.

LESSON 3-1

THE AMERICAN ECONOMY

The American economic system is made up of the inter-
changes among consumers, business, and government.

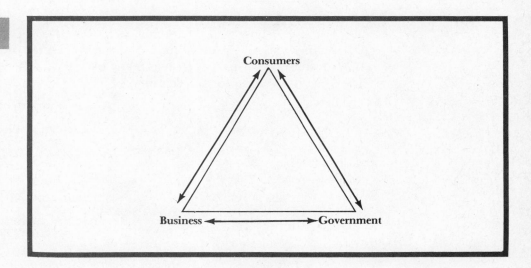

A **consumer** is anyone who buys goods and services. When resources,
income, materials, and labor are scarce, consumers have to give something up to get something else that they also want. There is a cost to every
economic decision you make. Therefore, **optimizing** your resources so that
your needs and wants are met is a worthwhile goal.

According to a U.S. government publication, *The American Economic System
. . . Your Part in It,** we make many economic decisions in our lives:

- Spending for things today or saving for the future

- Balancing spending for food, clothing, and shelter against spending for
  entertainment and recreation

- Undertaking extra work or spending that time on leisure activities

- Comparing the potential benefits of higher education with the costs and
  sacrifices it normally requires

The American Economic System . . . Your Part in It, 3rd printing, Pueblo, Colo., 1977,
United States Department of Labor.

1. Everyone contributes to the economy in some way. Cite an example of how you as a consumer contribute to the economy in

    (a) Your home _____

    (b) Your community _____

    (c) Your state _____

    (d) Your nation _____

2. Everyone benefits from government in some way. Cite an example of how you as a consumer benefit from the government.

    _____

    _____

    _____

3. Named below are items many teenagers want to own. You have been given $1,000.00 to spend on as many or as few of these items as you like. Put an "X" next to your selections.

    _____ television   _____ camping equipment

    _____ stereo   _____ own phone

    _____ class ring   _____ video cassette recorder

    _____ computer   _____ clothes

    _____ bicycle   _____ records and tapes

    _____ camera   _____ bedroom furniture

    _____ jewelry   _____ pet

    (a) Tell why you made the selection(s) you did.

    _____

    _____

    _____

    (b) What choices did you consider but give up to get what you wanted?

    _____

    _____

    _____

4. To **economize** means to use or manage your resources with thrift. Cite an example of how you might economize in obtaining one of your choices.

    _____

    _____

    _____

    _____

    _____

    _____

LESSON 3-2

BUYING GOODS AND SERVICES

Understanding the marketplace is essential to becoming a skilled consumer.

Consumers need businesses to **supply** (provide) **goods** (material items) and **services** (work performed for another). **Demand** is the willingness and ability of consumers to purchase goods and services at certain prices. Every consumer must decide what to buy and when and where to buy it. **Comparison shopping** means considering similar products and costs in order to get the best value.

1. Complete the goods and services comparison below by doing some comparison shopping in your community. Write the name of the business and the cost of each item, then place an "X" by the best buy in each category.

Goods/Services	Business 1	Business 2	Business 3
Large pepperoni pizza	Name: _____ Cost: $ _____	Name: _____ Cost: $ _____	Name: _____ Cost: $ _____
Haircut and blow-drying ...	Name: _____ Cost: $ _____	Name: _____ Cost: $ _____	Name: _____ Cost: $ _____
One gallon low-fat milk ...	Name: _____ Cost: $ _____	Name: _____ Cost: $ _____	Name: _____ Cost: $ _____
Drycleaning of a two-piece suit ..	Name: _____ Cost: $ _____	Name: _____ Cost: $ _____	Name: _____ Cost: $ _____
Hamburger and a cola	Name: _____ Cost: $ _____	Name: _____ Cost: $ _____	Name: _____ Cost: $ _____
Five gallons of unleaded gas ...	Name: _____ Cost: $ _____	Name: _____ Cost: $ _____	Name: _____ Cost: $ _____

Products and services that you buy should be things you value. Consumers learn what a good value is from advertising, from trial-and-error experiences, and from their families, friends, and neighbors.

2.   Describe a recent purchase in which you asked someone for advice. Are you happy with the purchase? Did you receive good advice? Did you consult any consumer guides, magazines, or advertisements before making the purchase?

_____

_____

_____

_____

_____

3.   Describe a situation in which you purchased a product or service without using comparison shopping. What was the outcome of this experience?

_____

_____

_____

_____

_____

4.   **Barter** is a popular way of trading goods and services without the exchange of money. For example, you might trade your talent in music by giving piano lessons for a ride to school every day. What talents, skills, services, or goods do you possess that you could use as barter?

_____

_____

_____

_____

_____

5.   Many career choices involve goods and services. Think about your future career and describe what goods or services you would like to provide.

_____

_____

_____

_____

_____

_____

_____

LESSON 3-3

THE TEENAGE CONSUMER

Children in the United States between the ages of six and sixteen spend over $50 billion a year.

Asurvey of 600 high school students showed that 72 percent earned their own money. The average student worked 13½ hours a week and earned an average weekly income of $42.00. Where did all of that money go? Surprisingly, the survey indicates that although teenagers are rich in personal possessions, most of their expensive belongings were paid for by their parents.

Study the graph below and answer the questions:

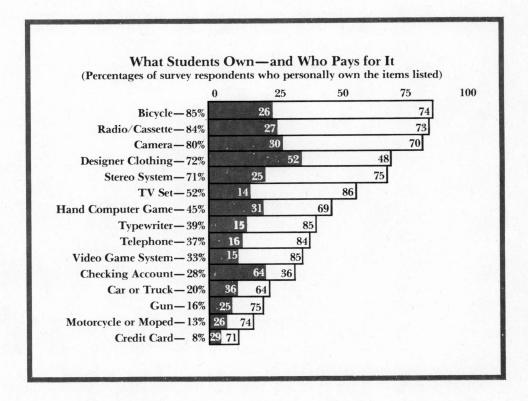

What Students Own—and Who Pays for It
(Percentages of survey respondents who personally own the items listed)

Item	Students	Parents
Bicycle—85%	26	74
Radio/Cassette—84%	27	73
Camera—80%	30	70
Designer Clothing—72%	52	48
Stereo System—71%	25	75
TV Set—52%	14	86
Hand Computer Game—45%	31	69
Typewriter—39%	15	85
Telephone—37%	16	84
Video Game System—33%	15	85
Checking Account—28%	64	36
Car or Truck—20%	36	64
Gun—16%	25	75
Motorcycle or Moped—13%	26	74
Credit Card—8%	29	71

How to read the graph: 85% of the students who answered our survey own a bicycle; 26% of those bicycles were paid for by the students; parents paid for the remaining 74% of the bicycles.

■ Percentage of students who paid for item.
□ Percentage of parents who paid for item.

Source: "Students and Their Money," *TeenAge Magazine*, Fall, 1982. Courtesy *TeenAge Magazine*, Bedford, MA. Copyright © by *Highwire Magazine*, 217 Jackson St., P.O. Box 948, Lowell, MA 01853. Reprinted by permission.

1.   What percentage of students had a car or truck? _____

2.   What percentage of parents paid for a bicycle? _____

3.   What percentage of students paid for a television set? _____

4.   What percentage of parents paid for a camera? _____

5.   What percentage of students had a credit card? _____

6.   Describe yourself as a wage earner and consumer. If you have a job, describe what you do, how many hours you work, your responsibilities, and the benefits you receive from working. As a consumer, what do you usually spend your money on? How do your earning and spending patterns differ from those reported in the survey?

_____

_____

_____

_____

_____

_____

_____

_____

_____

_____

_____

_____

_____

_____

_____

7.   Should teenagers who work ask their parents to pay for personal possessions? Explain your answer.

_____

_____

_____

_____

_____

_____

_____

_____

_____

LESSON 3-4

INFLATION

Inflation is a general rise in the cost of goods and services.

Today rising prices are a fact of life. In recent years inflation has been high. For example, with an annual inflation rate of 7 percent, a house that cost $50,000 in 1979 would cost $92,000 in 1988.

Smart shopping can help you beat inflation by increasing your buying power:

- Buy store or generic brands
- Shop sales
- Compare values, prices, and qualities
- Do not overpay for convenience such as aerosol cans, push-button containers, and fancy packaging
- Buy basic styles in clothing rather than fad fashions
- Buy foods in season
- Buy only what can be used and is needed

1. Name an item you purchased recently that you didn't need but wanted. Did you use any of the shopping tips listed above? Did you later find that there was something you needed more than this item?

   _____

   _____

   _____

2. (a) Name a product you buy regularly that has gone up in price.

   _____

   (b) What is the cheapest price you can recall paying for this item?

   _____

   (c) List two ways you could save money on the purchase if you wanted to buy this item today.

   _____

   _____

3.   Using Questions (a) through (g) below, interview an older person to find out how prices have changed in his or her lifetime.

   (a)   Do you remember what you paid for these items or services when you were a teenager?

   a newspaper $ _____   a soft drink $ _____

   a candy bar $ _____   a haircut $ _____

   a gallon of gas $ _____   a record $ _____

   (b)   Did you have a job when you were in school? _____

   Do you remember what you were paid? _____

   (c)   When you were a teenager what did you spend your money on?

   _____

   _____

   (d)   When you were a teenager what did you save money for?

   _____

   _____

   (e)   What items have increased the most in price since you were a teenager?

   _____

   _____

   (f)   Can you think of any items that have gone down in price?

   _____

   _____

   (g)   How has inflation affected what you buy?

   _____

   _____

4.   Compare the prices of the items listed in Question (a) with their prices today. Which items have increased the most in price?

   _____

   _____

   _____

   _____

   _____

   _____

   _____

   _____

   _____

   _____

   _____

LESSON 3-5

ADVERTISING

Advertising is the action of attracting public attention to a product or service.

Advertisers use various techniques to inform and entertain and to persuade consumers to buy what they are selling. For example, if an ad makes you want to be like someone else, it may be appealing to your emotions. If an ad is based upon reason and logic, it is probably appealing to your intelligence.

Effective advertising attracts your attention.

1. Choose an advertisement from a newspaper or magazine and analyze it:

    (a) What attracted you to the ad? _____

    (b) Where did you find the ad? _____

    (c) What is the ad selling? _____

    (d) Describe the audience for which the ad was designed:

    age _____ sex _____

    education level _____ race _____

    income _____ occupation _____

    interests _____

    (e) Describe how the ad appeals to the consumer's emotions or intelligence.

    _____

    _____

    _____

    _____

    (f) Do you think this ad would make consumers feel as if they need the product or service?

    _____

    _____

    _____

    _____

Television advertising often makes consumers believe that they will be healthier, happier, or more successful if they use a certain product or service. This type of advertising appeals to the ego, or self.

2. Write a television commercial that has ego appeal.

_____

_____

_____

_____

_____

_____

_____

_____

_____

_____

_____

_____

_____

_____

_____

_____

_____

_____

_____

_____

_____

_____

_____

_____

_____

LESSON 3-6

CONSUMER RIGHTS AND RESPONSIBILITIES

Consumers should understand and demand their rights
and should fulfill their responsibilities.

As a consumer and as a citizen you have certain rights and responsibilities.
A **right** is something you may properly claim is due you. A **responsibility**
is your duty to fulfill obligations and answer for your conduct.

In the preamble to his Consumer Message to Congress in March 1962, President John F. Kennedy proclaimed four basic consumer rights.

■   **The right to be informed** protects the consumer from fraudulent, deceitful or misleading information, advertising, and labeling. The consumer must be given the facts to make an informed choice. (The consumer is responsible for evaluating advertising, seeking additional information when needed, checking use instructions before buying, and reading warranties.)

■   **The right to choose** provides the consumer with a variety of products and services at competitive prices from which to choose. (The consumer is responsible for knowing what the choices are, doing as much comparison shopping as necessary, and resisting high-pressure sales tactics.)

■   **The right to safety** protects the consumer from goods and services which are hazardous to health and life. (The consumer is responsible for examining product safety features and studying instructions before buying or using the product.)

■   **The right to be heard** assures that consumer interests will be given full consideration in government policy. (The consumer is responsible for knowing where to seek help, suggesting and lobbying for consumer legislation, and expressing satisfaction or dissatisfaction with products and services.)

Study the following case studies and answer the questions:

1. Angel Alvarez has agreed to help her grandmother buy a new set of box springs and a mattress. They read in the newspaper that a nearby furniture store is having a bedding sale. Three differerent brands are advertised as being on sale. When they get to the store they find that only one brand of bedding is on sale. The salesperson urges them to buy it because "it's the best deal on bedding the store has had in years."

    (a)   What should Angel and her grandmother do? _____

    _____

    (b)   What consumer right are they exercising? _____

    _____

2. Tim Charles wants to earn extra money cutting firewood. He purchases a chain saw he has seen advertised on television. He is careful to read the directions and ask for help before he makes the purchase. After cutting down one small tree Tim notices that the safety guard is not working properly.

    (a)   What should Tim do? _____

    _____

    (b)   What consumer right is he exercising? _____

    _____

3. The Clark family goes on vacation and spends one night at the Villa Resort Hotel. They charge $68.34 on their bank card. When they receive their monthly statement they discover that the Villa Resort is listed with a $168.34 charge. The Clarks have their bank card receipt.

    (a)   What should the Clarks do? _____

    _____

    (b)   What consumer right are they exercising? _____

    _____

4. Marie Argo wants to lose weight quickly. A girlfriend suggests that she try Chocolate Diet Syrup. The product's advertisements give many testimonials from satisfied customers, but they do not list the ingredients in the product.

    (a)   What should Marie do? _____

    _____

    (b)   What consumer right is she exercising? _____

    _____

LESSON 3-7

REDRESS

Redress means to set right, remedy, rectify, correct, or adjust.

Have you ever purchased something only to find out later that the product or service is unsatisfactory? Consumers need to know how to seek redress and to let a business know that its products or service is unsatisfactory. When writing a letter of redress, the following information should be included:

- Your name, address, and phone number
- When and where the product or service was purchased
- Copies of sales receipts, guarantees, and warranties
- A brief statement concerning the problem
- Identifying factors for the product such as model number and style
- What you have done to resolve the problem
- What can be done to resolve the problem

Sample Letter of Redress

```
                                        101 51st Ave.
                                        New York, NY  10001-7821
                                        (212) 555-3221
                                        June 14, 1986

Department of Consumer Affairs
Explorations Media
1020 21st St.
San Francisco, CA  94010-2143


Dear Sir or Madam:

    Enclosed please find copies of my sales receipt for the purchase of video cassette
number 614 which I ordered from your catalog on April 1, 1986.  I have found the tape to
be defective.  I would like your company to either replace the tape or refund my money.

    I look forward to hearing from you.  Thank you.

                                        Sincerely,

                                        J. J. Jones
                                        J. J. Jones
```

Write a letter of redress about a real or imaginary product or service.

_____

_____

_____

_____

_____

_____

Dear

_____

_____

_____

_____

_____

_____

_____

_____

_____

_____

_____

_____

Sincerely,

LESSON 3-8

CONSUMER FRAUD

Frauds are deceptions, tricks, or practices designed to separate you from your money.

There are many different types of consumer fraud. Some frauds are illegal while others are simply misleading. Frauds are targeted at people who can least afford to lose money: the young, the old, the less educated, and the poor. Teenagers are often victims of frauds such as diet programs, muscle or bust development programs, get-rich-quick schemes, chain letters, acne treatments, correspondence schools, and used cars.

The best way to decide if a product or service is a fraud is to ask yourself these questions (if you answer "yes" to any of them, proceed with caution):

■   Does it seem too good to be true?

■   Does it seem too easy?

■   Do I have to hurry up and make a decision?

■   Is it going to cost me more money than I had intended to spend?

1.   Read the ad below and then answer the questions:

RID ACNE TREATMENT

Tired of unsightly red pimples? Tired of having no dates? Hate to look at yourself in the mirror? Then try the **Rid Acne** treatment. Guaranteed to get rid of all your acne in one week. Only $10.95 a jar. This extra low cost is available for a short time. Hurry, order today. Doctor tested, safe!

Rid Acne Treatment
405 West Ave. Clinic
Washington, D.C. 40872-9981

(a)   Does the Rid Acne Treatment seem too good to be true? _____

(b)   Why? _____

(c)   Does it seem too easy? _____

(d)   Does it require a quick decision? _____

(e)   Is it going to cost money? _____

2.   Look in a newspaper or magazine and find an ad that you feel is misleading. Paste or tape the ad in the box below.

```
┌─────────────────────────────────────────┐
│                                         │
│                                         │
│                                         │
│                                         │
│                                         │
│                                         │
│                                         │
│                                         │
│                                         │
│                                         │
└─────────────────────────────────────────┘
```

(a)   Does the ad suggest sales pressure? _____

(b)   Why might teenagers buy this product or service through the mail?

_____

_____

_____

_____

_____

_____

_____

_____

_____

(c)   Does the ad urge the consumer to hurry and make a decision?

_____

LESSON 3-9

SPENDING PLANS

A **spending plan** can guide your spending and help you achieve your financial goals.

Do you ever wonder where all your money goes? If you do, you could benefit from a spending plan. In developing a spending plan you must decide how much money you are going to spend on expenses such as food and entertainment, *before you spend it*.

To develop a spending plan you first need to estimate your fixed and variable expenses. **Fixed expenses** are those that occur regularly, such as bus fare or a weekly music lesson. **Variable expenses** are items with adjustable costs, such as entertainment, gifts, and snacks.

1. Use the charts below to keep an exact record of your money for two weeks. Record all income including allowance, salary, tips, gifts, and money from odd jobs. Record everything you buy, right down to the last hamburger!

Income and Expenses

	Week 1		Week 2	
	Planned	**Spent**	**Planned**	**Spent**
Weekly Expenses:	_____	_____	_____	_____
Fixed Expenses:				
Transportation	_____	_____	_____	_____
Lunches	_____	_____	_____	_____
Other	_____	_____	_____	_____
Variable Expenses:				
Clothing/grooming	_____	_____	_____	_____
Recreation	_____	_____	_____	_____
Hobbies	_____	_____	_____	_____
Gifts	_____	_____	_____	_____
Other	_____	_____	_____	_____
Total Weekly Expenses:	_____	_____	_____	_____

Weekly Income:
   Allowance .... $ _____
   Wages/tips .... $ _____
   Gifts .... $ _____
   Other .... $ _____
Total weekly income: .... $ _____

Your spending plan should be based not just on what you spend, but also on your financial goals. Once you have made a plan, you can set financial goals and see what your money can do for you.

2.   Evaluate your spending plan by answering these questions:

   (a)   Did you spend more money than you had planned? _____

   (b)   If so, what expenses did you underestimate? _____
         _____

   (c)   Was it more difficult to plan for your fixed or your flexible expenses?
         _____
         _____

   (d)   Were there any expenses you could have cut back on or eliminated?
         _____
         _____

   (e)   Were your expenses for Week 1 and Week 2 identical, similar, or
         very different? _____

3.   List five ways you would consider spending money differently in the future. If you would not make any changes, go on to the next question.

   _____
   _____
   _____
   _____
   _____
   _____
   _____
   _____
   _____

4.   If you do not plan to change your spending patterns, explain why your present plan is satisfactory.

   _____
   _____
   _____
   _____
   _____
   _____
   _____
   _____

LESSON 3-10

FINANCIAL GOALS

Financial goals are end results you are working to achieve through using your economic resources.

No individuals have the same financial goals, because no two individuals spend money in exactly the same way. Your financial goals change as your needs and wants change. An example of a long-term financial goal would be saving for a car; a short-term goal would be saving for clothing or dates.

1. List below several short-term (days or weeks) and long-term (year or more) financial goals:

Short-term	Long-term
_____	_____
_____	_____
_____	_____

2. Choose one of your short-term financial goals. Complete the statements and answer the following questions:

   (a) My financial goal is _____

   (b) The amount of money I estimate that I will need to achieve my goal is _____

   (c) What financial resources do you presently have that will help you achieve your goal?

   _____

   _____

   _____

   _____

   _____

   _____

   _____

(d) Describe the financial plan you will follow to help you achieve your goal.

_____

_____

_____

_____

_____

_____

_____

(e) How often will you save (daily, weekly, biweekly, monthly)?

_____

(f) Estimate how long it will take you to reach your goal.

_____

(g) What alternatives may you want to consider in working toward your goal?

_____

_____

_____

_____

_____

_____

(h) Keep a record of your progress toward your financial goal in the space below:

	Week 1	Week 2	Week 3	Week 4	Week 5
Totals:					

LESSON 3-11

SAVINGS ACCOUNTS

A **savings account** is a plan offered by a financial institution that pays interest on the amount of money deposited.

Saving money is one way to work toward achieving your financial goals. Where and how to save are important decisions. You might want to consider the following factors:

- **Safety:** What degree of risk are you taking that you might lose some or all of your money?

- **Availability:** How easily and quickly can you get your money? Will you have to pay a penalty for an early withdrawal?

- **Purpose:** How do you want to use this money?

- **Earnings:** How quickly will your money grow in value?

One way to save money is to use a regular passbook savings account. (A **passbook** is a record of the principal and interest.) This type of account is easily converted to cash. You can make a withdrawal any time without paying a penalty.

The **principal** is the amount of money invested by the **depositor** (saver). The **interest** is the money paid by the bank to the saver for the use of the money. When interest is computed on the sum of the principal plus the interest already earned, it is called **compound interest**. The table illustrates how annual interest is compounded on a passbook savings account.

Use the table to answer the following question.

1. If you deposited $100.00 and left it in the bank for three years at 5½ percent annual interest **rate**, you would have a balance of _____ .

Year	Beginning Balance	Interest Earned (5½ Percent)	Ending Balance
1	$100.00	$5.50	$105.50
2	$105.50	$5.80	$111.30
3	$111.30	$6.12	$117.42

A second way to save money is to invest in a **certificate of deposit**. This savings plan requires a minimum deposit, usually $500.00. A certificate of deposit has the advantage of earning more interest than a passbook account. However, if you make a withdrawal before the set **maturity date** (required period of deposit, or set date of withdrawal), you will have to pay a penalty.

2. Jared is trying to figure out how much money he will have if he deposits $500.00 in a regular passbook account paying 5 percent interest. Calculate how much he will have at the end of each year using compound interest:

   (a) First Year _____ (b) Second Year _____ (c) Third Year _____

3. How much will Jared have at the end of three years if he deposits the $500.00 in a certificate of deposit paying 7 percent compounded annual interest?

   _____

4. Match the following terms and identifying phrases:

   Answers

   a. passbook
   b. inflation
   c. compound interest
   d. depositor
   e. maturity date
   f. principal
   g. certificate of deposit
   h. interest
   i. rate

   1. when interest is computed on the sum of the principal plus interest already earned ....   1. _____

   2. interest expressed as a percentage ....   2. _____

   3. the amount paid for the use of money ....   3. _____

   4. a record of the principal and interest ....   4. _____

   5. a person who opens a savings account ....   5. _____

   6. a savings plan that limits withdrawals ....   6. _____

   7. a general rise in the cost of goods and services ....   7. _____

   8. a set date of withdrawal ....   8. _____

   9. the amount on which interest is computed ....   9. _____

LESSON 3-12

ESTABLISHING CREDIT

Credit is the ability to buy something now and pay for it later.

Credit is not more money. Credit is the use of someone else's money. The use of credit makes it possible to have the things you need and want without using cash. A lender usually considers three factors before issuing credit:

- Your ability to repay a loan based upon your income and other expenses

- Your **assets** (what you already own)

- Your **credit history** (your record of making payments on time establishes you as a good credit risk)

To build your credit history you may want to obtain a credit card or a loan. Credit cards help you purchase goods and services and pay for them later. A **loan** is an advancement of money which you can then use to purchase goods and services. If you have not established a credit history, you may need a cosigner for a loan. A **cosigner** is someone who signs the note with you and is responsible for the loan repayment if you **default** (can't make the payments).

1. Why is it important to establish a good credit history?

_____

_____

_____

_____

2. In most states the legal age for opening a charge account or obtaining a loan is eighteen. Would you recommend that the age limit be raised? Why or why not?

_____

_____

_____

_____

_____

3.   What does it mean to be a "good credit risk"?

_____

_____

_____

_____

_____

_____

4.   Americans are said to live in a "cashless society." What does this mean?

_____

_____

_____

_____

_____

_____

5.   Why is there risk involved in being a cosigner on a loan?

_____

_____

_____

_____

_____

_____

6.   Mike and Denise are a young married couple. Their combined incomes provide a comfortable lifestyle for them. Both Mike and Denise have been taught to pay cash for everything and to save money for large items. They would like to buy a home in a few years and will need to borrow the money. What credit advice would you give them?

_____

_____

_____

_____

_____

_____

_____

_____

LESSON 3-13

CREDIT ACCOUNTS

Financial experts suggest that individuals should not spend more than 20 percent of their monthly income on credit payments.

Credit isn't free. It is paid for by interest charges that vary with the type of credit, the borrower's credit history, and the time period involved. The wise consumer is familiar with the types of credit accounts and interest charges.

Regular or 30-day accounts require that a consumer pay the amount due in full each month. No finance charge is required if payments are made on time.

Revolving or open-ended accounts allow the consumer to repay the debt monthly in full with no finance charge or to make a partial payment each month, in which case there is a finance charge. MasterCard and Visa operate on a revolving basis. A credit line or limit is established for the consumer.

Installment accounts require that consumers repay the amount owed in a specific number of payments over a certain amount of time. A downpayment is usually required. Expensive items such as appliances, furniture, and cars are most often bought on installment accounts.

1. Why might a consumer use credit accounts and charge purchases rather than pay cash?

    _____

    _____

    _____

    _____

    _____

2.   Read each statement below and identify the type of credit that would best satisfy these consumers' needs:

(a)   Martha wants to earn money mowing lawns, but she will have to purchase a new lawnmower. She cannot afford to pay cash for the mower, but she does have enough money for a downpayment. What type of credit might be best for Martha?

_____

(b)   Carmen wants to buy a pair of snow skis. She sees just what she wants advertised in an "August special." What types of credit accounts might she use so that she will have the skis when winter comes?

_____

(c)   Keiko has been taking violin lessons for ten years. Her teacher suggests that she needs a better instrument. The music store will let Keiko's parents buy a new violin on a revolving account. What does this mean?

_____

_____

(d)   Steven wants to open a regular charge account at Bunk's Department Store. Steven knows that he will have to pay each month's balance in full. What will happen if he cannot pay the total balance?

_____

_____

(e)   Sherry will be needing a car to get to her after-school job. Her dad tells her that he will make the downpayment but that she will have to make the monthly payments. The car salesperson says the APR on the car she wants is eight percent. What does this mean?

_____

_____

(f)   The Meddler family has a revolving charge account in a clothing store. With an 18 percent APR, what would the finance charge be on a $200.00 balance carried throughout the year?

_____

LESSON 3-14

FEDERAL CREDIT LAWS

Consumers are protected from unprincipled practices on the part of lenders by several federal laws.

Fair Credit Reporting Act (1971) assures consumers of fair treatment by credit reporting agencies. This law ensures that the credit report on a consumer is accurate and that it is used in a confidential manner. This law guarantees your right to know what is in your credit file.

Equal Credit Opportunity Act (1975, 1977) prohibits discrimination against a credit applicant based on sex, marital status, religion, race, national origin, or receipt of public assistance. If you feel you have been discriminated against, you have the right to inspect your credit file.

Consumer Credit Protection Act (1969), also known as the Truth-in-Lending Law, is designed to assure that consumers are informed about credit terms. The consumer must be told the dollar amount and the annual percentage rate (APR) before credit can be extended. This law also limits a credit card holder's liability for unauthorized use to $50.00 per card.

Fair Credit Billing Act (1975) protects a consumer's credit rating when there is a dispute about the amount owed on a credit card or revolving credit purchase. The law gives consumers the opportunity to correct errors which may appear on their billing statements without damaging their credit rating.

Cash Discount Act (1981) encourages retailers nationwide to offer lower prices to their customers who pay in cash. Credit must be paid for just as other services are paid for; that is why purchases made with credit usually cost more.

Read each statement below and identify the credit law that protects the consumer:

Answers

1. Michael has lost his credit card. According to the Consumer Credit Protection Act, he is liable for $ ___?___ if someone else uses the card. ....

    1. _____

2. Lindsay wants to buy a car and wants to know more about the credit terms. She can get this information because of the ___?___ Act. ....

    2. _____

    _____

(continued)

3. James has just received a letter stating that his credit application has been turned down. He feels that he has been discriminated against. He is protected by the _____?_____ Act. ....

3. _____

   _____

4. Sean wants to know what is in his credit file. He has the right to know this information because he is protected by the _____?_____ Act. ....

4. _____

   _____

5. Beth and Joe want to purchase $2,000.00 worth of lumber to build a deck and patio. They plan to pay cash and do some comparison shopping to find a retailer who offers a discount for cash. They are aware of the _____?_____ Act. ....

5. _____

   _____

6. Duane is shopping for a stereo. Store A will finance the purchase at an APR of 18 percent. Store B will finance the same stereo at an APR of 20 percent. He will have no difficulty determining which charges the higher rate for each dollar of credit because of the _____?_____ Act. ....

6. _____

   _____

7. Ellie is certain that her favorite department store has made an error in her monthly billing statement. She isn't too worried, however, because she knows she has 60 days to register a written complaint. Her good credit rating is protected by the _____?_____ Act. ....

7. _____

   _____

8. Mary wants to borrow money for a car. She is recently divorced. Her marital status cannot affect the loan because of the _____?_____ Act. ....

8. _____

   _____

LESSON 3-15

CHECKING ACCOUNTS: PERSONAL CHECKS

A **checking account** is a way of paying for the things you buy without carrying cash or using credit.

A personal check is a written order directing the bank to subtract money from your account. A canceled check is legal proof of payment.

The person who opens a checking account or writes a check is called a **drawer** or **payor**. The person to whom the check is written is the **payee**. Checks are always written in ink so that they cannot be changed.

Below is an example of a personal check.

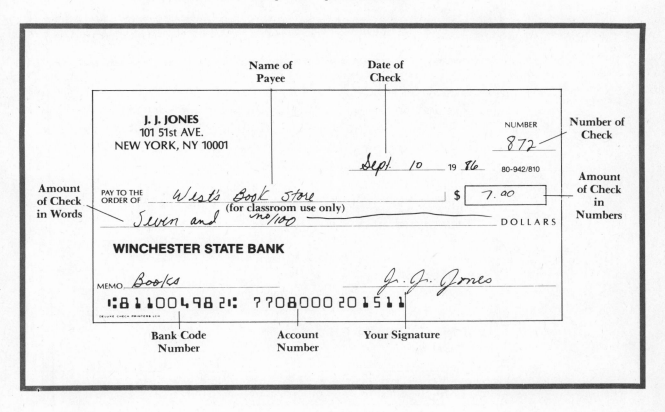

The amount of money you have in your account is called the **balance**. A **check register** or **check stub** is your record of your balance—what you put into and pay out of your checking account. You cannot write checks for more money than you have in your account. If you do, the account will be **overdrawn** and the bank will charge you a fee for writing a bad check.

1. Below is an example of a check register. What is the current balance?

    _____

Check No.	Date	Description	Codes P	T	Check Amount	✔	Deposits	Balance Forward
								179 93
	11-08	Deposit					75 00	254 93
52	11-08	The Gift Basket Andy's Present			7 00			247 93
53	12-18	ABC Hardware Lumber			50 00			197 93
54	12-18	Mary Lyn's Boutique Scarf			13 00			184 93

2. Write a check for $17.50 to Picture Perfect Framing and record what you have done in the register above. What is the new balance?

    _____

SUSAN MARLOWE
1116 ST. MARIE AVE.
SPRINGFIELD, OH

NUMBER

_____ 19____   80-942/810

PAY TO THE
ORDER OF _____ $ [   ]
                 (for classroom use only)

_____ DOLLARS

WINCHESTER STATE BANK

MEMO _____   _____

⑆811004982⑆ 7708000201511

LESSON 3-16

CHECKING ACCOUNTS: DEPOSITS AND WITHDRAWALS

A **deposit** is a written order directing the bank to add money to your account.

A deposit slip is used to deposit checks and cash into an account. Below is an example of a deposit slip:

Amount of Coins Deposited

Amount of Paper Money Deposited

DEPOSIT TICKET

NAME_____

ACCOUNT NO._____

DATE_____ 19 _____

SIGN HERE FOR CASH RECEIVED (IF REQUIRED)

WINCHESTER STATE BANK

CASH	CURRENCY		
	COIN		
LIST CHECKS SINGLY			
			80-459/810
TOTAL FROM OTHER SIDE			
TOTAL			USE OTHER SIDE FOR ADDITIONAL LISTING
LESS CASH RECEIVED			
NET DEPOSIT			BE SURE EACH ITEM IS PROPERLY ENDORSED

Amount of Each Check Deposited

Cash Received (If Any)

Total Deposit (Less Cash)

⑆8⑈⑈0049 8 2⑆ 770 8000 20 1 5 ⑈ ⑈

CHECKS AND OTHER ITEMS ARE RECEIVED FOR DEPOSIT SUBJECT TO THE PROVISIONS OF THE UNIFORM COMMERCIAL CODE OR ANY APPLICABLE COLLECTION AGREEMENT

Bank Code   Account Number   Total: Checks, Coins and Currency Deposited

1. Complete the deposit slip on the following page for J. David Austin. He wants to deposit $7.00 in coin and checks in the amounts of $89.23, $33.00, and $4.19. He wants $15.00 back in cash.

```
DEPOSIT TICKET
```

NAME _____

CASH	CURRENCY		
	COIN		
LIST CHECKS SINGLY		

DATE _____ 19 _____

TOTAL FROM OTHER SIDE		
TOTAL		
► LESS CASH RECEIVED		
NET DEPOSIT		

80-459/810

USE OTHER SIDE FOR
ADDITIONAL LISTING

BE SURE EACH ITEM IS
PROPERLY ENDORSED

_____
SIGN HERE FOR CASH RECEIVED (IF REQUIRED)

WINCHESTER STATE BANK

⑆81100498 2⑆   7708000 201511

CHECKS AND OTHER ITEMS ARE RECEIVED FOR DEPOSIT SUBJECT TO THE PROVISIONS OF THE UNIFORM COMMERCIAL CODE OR ANY APPLICABLE COLLECTION AGREEMENT

A **withdrawal slip** is used to take money out of an account. Below is an example of a withdrawal slip:

2.   Complete a withdrawal slip for Valerie Green. Her account number is 472-100089. She wants to withdraw a total of $110.00. She wants $30.00 in cash and a bank check for $80.00.

WINCHESTER STATE BANK   **SAVINGS WITHDRAWAL**

ACCOUNT NUMBER

Date _____ 19 _____

THE SUM OF _____ $ _____
Authorized   (Write Amount in Words)   (Write Amount in Figures)
Signature _____
                    (for classroom use only)

Print Name _____

Address _____

⑆81100498 2⑆   7708000 201511

LESSON 3-17

BANK STATEMENT

A **bank statement** is the bank's record of your checking account.

Each month your bank will send a statement of your account including all of your cancelled checks and deposit slips. To **balance** or **reconcile** your checkbook you must compare your checkbook balance with the bank's statement. The checks and deposits that aren't shown on your bank statement but that you have recorded in your checkbook are called **outstanding**. Many banks charge a fee called a **service charge**. This fee will be shown on your bank statement.

Statement					**WINCHESTER STATE BANK**

SUSAN MARLOWE
1116 ST. MARIE AVE.
SPRINGFIELD, OH

Reference Number	130421456	Page Number	1

Statement Date

Statement Instructions | 12-04-86

Beginning Balance	No. of Deposits and Credits	We have added these deposits and credits totaling	No. of Withdrawals and Charges	We have subtracted these withdrawals and charges totaling	Resulting in a statement balance of
179.93	2	200.00	4	91.56	282.37

Document Count	Average daily balance this statement period		Minimum balance this statement period	Date	Amount
7					

If your account does not balance, please see reverse side and report any discrepancy to our Customer Service Department ▶

Previous Statement

Date	Amount	Description	Balance
11-08	75.00	Deposit	254.93
11-12	125.00	Deposit	379.93
11-08	7.00	Check	372.93
11-15	21.06	Check	351.87
11-18	50.00	Check	301.87
12-04	13.50	Check	288.37
12-04	6.00	Service Chg.	282.37

1. What was the balance at the beginning of the summary period?

    _____

2. What is the current balance? _____

3. Checks written after _____ would not appear on this bank statement.

4. The total amount of credits was _____ , and the total amount of debits was _____ .

Reconcile your checking account using the bank statement above. You made a $133.17 deposit this morning. Your check register shows that three checks are outstanding: Check No. 78 for $34.92; Check No. 80 for $9.00; and Check No. 81 for $42.50. After subtracting the bank's service charge your current balance is $323.12.

Follow the steps below to balance your checking account statement:

Present balance shown on statement: $ _____

Add deposits not shown
on this statement (if any): $ _____

Total: $ _____

Subtract checks outstanding and
service charges (if any): $ _____

Balance—this amount should agree
with your checkbook balance: $ _____

Checks Outstanding

No.	Amount	
78	$ 34	92
80	9	00
81	42	50
Total		

If your account does not balance, please check the following carefully:

[   ] Have you correctly entered the amount of each check and debit on your checkbook register?

[   ] Are the amounts of your deposits and credits entered on the checkbook register the same as in your statement?

[   ] Have all advances and automatic transfers been entered in your register?

[   ] Have all checks been deducted from your register?

[   ] Have you deducted all bank charges and other debits from your register?

[   ] Have you carried the correct balance forward from each checkbook register to the next?

[   ] Have you checked all additions and subtractions on your checkbook register?

[   ] Have you earned any interest which needs to be added to your balance?

LESSON 3-18

ASSETS AND LIABILITIES

Assets are the dollar value of what you own. **Liabilities** are the dollar value of what you owe.

Examples of financial assets include but are not limited to:

- Cash (checking accounts, savings, and money market funds)
- Life insurance (cash value only)
- Investments (stocks, bonds, real estate)
- Personal belongings (clothing, jewelry, tools, car)

Examples of financial liabilities include but are not limited to:

- Personal loans (money owed to others)
- Charge accounts (department store accounts)
- Credit card accounts (MasterCard or Visa)
- Unpaid bills (rent, utilities, phone, taxes)

Net worth is the difference between your assets and your liabilities. The following exercise is designed so that you can determine your own net worth:

What You Own (assets)	Amount
Cash in checking accounts	$ _____
Cash in savings accounts	_____
Current value of government bonds	_____
Cash value of life insurance policies	_____
Loans owed you	_____
Tax refunds owed you	_____
Market value of stocks, bonds, trusts	_____
Cash value of personal belongings	_____
Car	_____
Clothing	_____
Sporting equipment	_____
Stereo, television	_____
Furniture	_____
Records, books	_____
Jewelry, art	_____
Other assets	_____
Total of what you own:	$ _____

What You Owe (liabilities)	Amount
Installment debts (credit cards, charge accounts, balance due on car)	$ _____
Personal loans	_____
Current bills outstanding	_____
Taxes due	_____
Other liabilities	_____
Total of what you owe:	$ _____
Your Net Worth (assets minus liabilities)	$ _____

1. What have you learned from figuring your net worth?

    _____

    _____

    _____

    _____

    _____

    _____

2. Are your financial goals going to change or remain the same?

    _____

    _____

    _____

    _____

    _____

    _____

UNIT 4

FOODS AND NUTRITION: YOU AND GOOD EATING

UNIT 4

OBJECTIVES:

This unit provides information that will help you to:

■ Define the "Basic Four Food Groups"

■ Choose a balanced diet to meet body needs

■ Explain the relationships among caloric intake, body weight, diet, and health

■ Interpret information on food labels

■ Practice food shopping skills

■ Plan and prepare meals that provide balanced nutrition

No other country in the world produces more food than the United States, yet an abundance of food has not eliminated hunger and poor nutrition from our society. Millions of Americans suffer from diet-related health problems such as heart disease, obesity, and diabetes.

Nutrition is a complex subject. There is no one answer to the often-asked question "What should I eat?" because no two people have exactly the same nutritional needs, physical activity level, or food preferences. Eating well and staying healthy require many decisions. One way to become more conscious of your own food decisions is to keep a record of everything you eat in a 24-hour period. You will be surprised at how many choices and decisions you make. To be well nourished, choose a variety of foods containing the essential nutrients—protein, carbohydrates, minerals, vitamins, fats, and water—from the Basic Four Food Groups.

There is more to food and nutrition than eating a balanced diet, however. People eat not only to satisfy hunger, but also to fulfill social, emotional, and cultural needs. Personal values and available resources such as time, energy, space, and equipment often determine the foods we buy. And that very important resource, money, is always an important factor in deciding what to eat and where to buy food. The lessons in this unit will help you understand how to choose food that will provide you with adequate nutrition and will give you an opportunity to practice decision-making in shopping, planning, and preparing food.

LESSON 4-1

NUTRITION: THE BASICS

Food provides the energy and nutrients your body needs
to function properly. Wise food choices lead to healthier,
stronger bodies.

Nutrition information helps you evaluate food fads, fallacies, and other
food claims. There are no miracle foods, fast diets, or special pills. To be
well nourished and healthy, you need to eat a combination of foods every day
from each of **the Basic Four Food Groups**. Below are the recommended
numbers of servings per food group, along with examples of special foods:

■   Four servings from **milk group** (six servings if you are pregnant) — milk,
     cheese, ice cream, yogurt

■   Two servings from the **meat group** (three servings if you are pregnant) —
     beef, chicken, fish, eggs

■   Four servings from the **grain group** — bread, cereal, pancakes, rice

■   Four servings from the **fruit and vegetable group** — potatoes, watermelon,
     okra, beans

1.   List the foods you have eaten today in the appropriate spaces.

Milk	Meat

Grain	Fruit and Vegetables

2.   Was your diet for today balanced? That is, are you getting adequate amounts (servings) from each food group? If not, how should you change your diet?

_____

_____

_____

3.   What would be wrong with a grapefruit diet which consisted of eating five grapefruits a day and drinking only water?

_____

_____

_____

4.   Some foods include nutrients from two or more food groups. List the basic food groups included in the following foods.

(a)   Strawberry milkshake _____

_____

(b)   Cheeseburger _____

_____

(c)   Taco _____

_____

(d)   Bagels and cream cheese _____

_____

(e)   Red beans and rice _____

_____

5.   A recent census showed that 40 percent of the average family's food budget went to fast food restaurants. Which foods commonly sold in fast food restaurants would give you the most nutrients at the lowest price? Check local restaurants' menus if necessary.

_____

_____

_____

_____

_____

_____

_____

_____

_____

_____

LESSON 4-2

NUTRITION: FOOD COMPOSITION

Nutrients are substances or ingredients which provide nourishment. Nourishment gives energy for activities as well as growth.

Your body needs 50 or more nutrients. Each nutrient has a special function. No single food supplies all the nutrients your body needs; therefore, you need to eat a variety of foods from the Basic Four Food Groups each day. Ten nutrients are considered to be particularly essential.

The Terrific Ten

- Protein builds and repairs body tissue and supplies energy. Sources include meat, cheese, milk products, and fish.

- Carbohydrates energize you and supply fiber. Sources include lettuce, tomatoes, rolls, pasta, grains, vegetables, and fruits.

- Lipids (fats) energize you and carry vitamins A, D, C, and K in the body. Without fat your body would have difficulty utilizing these vitamins. Sources include fat in meat, milk products, and salad dressings.

- Vitamin A aids vision, keeps skin healthy, and fights off infections. Sources include fruits and vegetables.

- Vitamin C helps fight off infections, heals cuts, and forms collagen (a cementing substance which holds the cells together). Sources include fruits and vegetables, especially citrus fruits, strawberries, broccoli, and bananas.

- Thiamin helps your digestive and nervous systems function properly and helps your body use energy. Sources include grain products, meat, fruits, and vegetables.

- Riboflavin keeps skin healthy, aids vision, and helps you use energy. Sources include cheese, meat, and milk products.

- Niacin is good for healthy skin, helps your body use energy, and is good for your appetite and digestion. Sources include meat and grains.

- Calcium strengthens bones and teeth, is good for muscles, and helps your blood clot. Sources include milk products and cheese.

- Iron prevents infections, anemia, and fatigue, and helps your body use glucose. Sources include red meat and grain products.

1. You want a sandwich for lunch. This sandwich must contain all of the Terrific Ten nutrients. Build a sandwich, labeling the layers.

Bread

_____

_____

_____

_____

_____

_____

_____

_____

_____

Bread

2. Jana has been told by her doctor that she is slightly anemic and needs to add more iron-rich foods to her diet. What should she eat?

_____

_____

_____

_____

3. Bill's coach has suggested that before he runs in the Boston Marathon he should "load up" on carbohydrates. What should he eat?

_____

_____

_____

_____

LESSON 4-3

LOSING, MAINTAINING, AND GAINING WEIGHT

To reach your ideal weight you should balance what you eat with what your body uses.

It is difficult to judge your ideal weight by using height and weight charts alone, because you also have to consider your bone density, muscle tone, and amount of body fat. Muscle weighs more than fat, so athletes would probably have better muscle tone and weigh more than non-athletes. The safest way to influence your weight is to control your diet and to exercise.

- To lose weight you have to eat less each day than your average daily calorie output. The average 15- to 18-year-old female uses about 18 calories per day per pound of fat weight (the number of calories varies because of exercise). The average 15- to 18-year-old male uses about 19 calories per day per pound of body weight.

- To maintain weight you have to eat as many calories as your body uses.

- To gain weight you have to eat more calories per day than you use. If you are extremely active, you may have to exercise less to gain weight.

Recommended Daily Calorie Intake Chart

Age	Calories for Males	Calories for Females
11-14	2700	2200
15-18	2800	2100
19-22	2900	2100
23-50	2700	2000
51-75	2400	1800
75+	2050	1600

Source: Food and Nutrition Board, National Academy of Science, National Research Council, *Recommended Dietary Allowances*, ed. 9 (Washington, D.C.: National Academy Press, 1980).

1. Why can't you rely completely on height, weight, and calorie charts to figure your ideal weight?

_____

_____

2. Look at the advertisement below and answer the questions that follow:

SANDMAN WEIGHT LOSS PLAN

Try the new nighttime weight loss plan today! Lose ten pounds in one week. No exercise required. Eat all your favorite foods. No more starving. No expensive pills or vitamins. Just wear the special weight-loss pajamas nightly. Lose weight while you sleep. The pajamas are comfortable and machine washable. One size fits all. Only $19.95 postpaid. Doctor tested and recommended. Send check or money order to:

The Sandman Weight Loss Plan
North Plains Diet Institute
St. Cloud, MN 45361-0127

Does this plan:

		Yes	No	Not Sure
(a)	Recommend exercise?	_____	_____	_____
(b)	Recommend dietary changes? ...	_____	_____	_____
(c)	Recommend the use of pills?	_____	_____	_____
(d)	Recommend a doctor's examination before beginning?	_____	_____	_____
(e)	Recommend vitamins?	_____	_____	_____
(f)	Include all the foods you like to eat?	_____	_____	_____
(g)	Help you develop better eating patterns?	_____	_____	_____
(h)	Adapt to your lifestyle?	_____	_____	_____
(i)	Tell you which doctors recommend the plan?	_____	_____	_____
(j)	Offer a money-back guarantee? ..	_____	_____	_____
(k)	Seem logical and workable to you?	_____	_____	_____

Why or why not? _____

_____

_____

_____

LESSON 4-4

FOOD CHOICES

Food choices affect your energy, growth, alertness, and sense of well-being.

The U.S. Senate Select Committee has provided the following suggestions for food choices:*

- **Eat a variety of foods daily:** Include these foods every day in your diet: fruits and vegetables, whole grain and enriched breads and cereals, milk and milk products, meats, fish, poultry, eggs, and dried peas and beans.

- **Maintain ideal weight:** Increase physical activity. Reduce calories by eating fewer fatty foods and sweets and less sugar. Avoid alcohol. Lose weight gradually.

- **Avoid too much fat, saturated fat, and cholesterol:** Choose low-fat protein sources such as lean meats, fish, poultry, dried peas, and beans. Use eggs and organ meats in moderation. Limit intake of fats on and in foods. Trim fats from meats. Broil, bake, or boil—don't fry. Read food labels for fat contents.

- **Eat foods with adequate starch and fiber:** Substitute starches for fats and sugars. Select whole grain breads and cereal, fruits and vegetables, dried peas and beans, and nuts to increase fiber and starch intake.

- **Avoid too much sugar:** Use less sugar, syrup, and honey. Reduce concentrated sweets such as candy, soft drinks, and cookies. Select fresh fruits or fruits canned in light syrup or their own juices. Read food labels: sucrose, glucose, dextrose, maltose, lactose, fructose, syrups, and honey are all sugars. Eat sugar less often to reduce dental cavities.

- **Avoid too much sodium:** Reduce salt in cooking. Add little or no salt at the table. Limit salty foods such as potato chips, pretzels, salted nuts, popcorn, condiments, cheese, pickled foods, and cured meats. Read food labels for sodium or salt contents, especially in processed and snack foods.

- **If you drink alcohol, do so in moderation:** Individuals who drink should limit all alcoholic beverages (including wine, beer, and liquors). *Note:* Consumption of alcoholic beverages during pregnancy can result in the development of birth defects and mental retardation called **fetal alcohol syndrome.**

*Source: Adapted from U.S. Senate Select Committee on Nutrition and Human Needs, *Dietary Goals for the United States*, 2nd ed. (Washington, D.C.: U.S. Government Printing Office, December 1977).

1. In the food intake diary below, list everything you eat for three days. Include approximate amounts—for example, "large glass of orange juice," "two glazed doughnuts."

Food Intake Diary

Date:	Date:	Date:
Morning:	*Morning:*	*Morning:*
Afternoon:	*Afternoon:*	*Afternoon:*
Evening:	*Evening:*	*Evening:*

(a) Were these three days typical of your usual food intake? _____

(b) Why or why not? _____

2. Review the suggestions for food choices and evaluate your diet as listed in the diary. Place an "X" in the column that best describes the amounts of food types you consume.

Food Type	Amounts		
	Too High	About Right	Too Low
Fats, cholesterol	_____	_____	_____
Sugar	_____	_____	_____
Starch, fiber	_____	_____	_____
Sodium	_____	_____	_____

LESSON 4-5

FAST FOODS

Teenagers are frequent customers of the over 150,000 fast food restaurants in the United States.

Fast food restaurants are popular because they are convenient, predictable, fast, and usually inexpensive.

Is fast food good for you? Yes, if you make the right choices, and if you consider how the fast food meal fits into your total daily food intake. Nutritionists point out that many fast food meals are:

■ Low in vitamins A and C

■ Low in calcium

■ High in calories

■ Low in fiber

You can add vitamins A and C and fiber by:

■ Choosing salads

■ Adding lettuce and tomato to your hamburger

■ Choosing whole grain breads

■ Drinking orange juice (vitamin C)

You can add calcium by:

■ Having pizza (with cheese)

■ Drinking milk or a milkshake made with whole milk

■ Eating ice cream or yogurt

■ Choosing a cheeseburger over a plain hamburger

You can reduce calories by:

■ Choosing diet dressings for salad

■ Ordering diet soft drinks

■ Avoiding gravy, french fries, dessert pies, and fried foods

■ Eating smaller portions

Keeping in mind the hints above and the Basic Four Food Groups (milk, meat, fruits/vegetables, grains), list the pros, cons, and corrections for each of the fast food meals below to make them more balanced.

1. Meal 1: Fried chicken, mashed potatoes, biscuit, coleslaw, fried cherry turnover, milk

    (a) Pros _____

    (b) Cons _____

    (c) Corrections _____

2. Meal 2: Hamburger, french fries, soft drink

    (a) Pros _____

    (b) Cons _____

    (c) Corrections _____

3. Meal 3: "Everything on it" pizza, iced tea

    (a) Pros _____

    (b) Cons _____

    (c) Corrections _____

4. Meal 4: Roast beef sandwich, salad bar, diet cola

    (a) Pros _____

    (b) Cons _____

    (c) Corrections _____

5. Allison had orange juice for breakfast, and a plain hamburger, french fries, and a soft drink for lunch. What should she eat for dinner to help balance her food intake for the day? (She wants to maintain her present weight.)

    _____

    _____

    _____

LESSON 4-6

EATING DISORDERS

Two eating disorders, anorexia nervosa and bulimia, are related to weight loss and are particular problems for adolescents.

Anorexia nervosa is an extreme preoccupation with weight loss which endangers the life and health of one percent of all 16- to 18-year-olds. Usually the anorexic starts dieting to lose a little weight and then cannot stop. The person is often from a well-educated, middle-class, success-oriented, weight-conscious family. The weight can go as low as 65 to 70 pounds, which is at the life-threatening level for anyone of average height. Treatment requires a skilled physician who oversees a process in which normal nutrition is gradually restored.

Bulimia is periodic binge eating alternating with intervals of dieting or self-starvation. The bulimic eats a large quantity of food and then induces vomiting or takes laxatives. Although bulimia is rarely life-threatening, it is damaging to the stomach and the esophagus and leads to malnutrition (with other resulting physical effects).

With both eating disorders, the emotional support provided by the adolescent's family and friends is important for recovery, but the person must want to change his or her eating habits in order for treatment to succeed.

1. It is less common for boys to have anorexia or bulimia. How would you explain this?

    _____

    _____

    _____

2. Judith's best friend, Autumn, has eaten only one-half piece of dry toast for breakfast, nothing for lunch or snacks, and only lettuce and carrots for dinner for over a month. Autumn has been telling her parents that she eats a lot for lunch and after school and isn't hungry, so her parents aren't worried. Judith is afraid that Autumn has _____ and is not sure what to do. What can Judith do to help Autumn?

    _____

    _____

3.   What is wrong with the saying "You can never be too thin"?

_____

_____

_____

_____

_____

4.   Malnourished adolescents are likely to be listless, tired, inattentive, or irritable because they don't feel well. How will being an anorexic or bulimic affect the student's ability to:

(a)   Do schoolwork?

_____

_____

_____

(b)   Play volleyball?

_____

_____

_____

(c)   Work in a day care center?

_____

_____

_____

(d)   Act in the school play?

_____

_____

_____

(e)   Get along with family members?

_____

_____

_____

5.   Do you think the media (television, magazines, newspapers, movies) encourage us to look a certain way? What way is popular now (hairstyle, clothes, weight/figure)?

_____

_____

_____

_____

_____

LESSON 4-7

FOODS, MOODS, AND ATTITUDES

Food does more than provide nourishment for the body. Many of our food choices are influenced by our moods, attitudes, and beliefs.

Food is associated with feelings of closeness, dependence, and comfort. This is why most people prefer to eat with others. Food can help us manage stress, sadness, boredom, or depression. When you are ill or unhappy certain foods may seem more soothing and appealing. Food can also serve as a symbol of friendship through sharing and gift giving.

Fill in the blanks with the first food that comes to mind. Place your answer in the answer column at the right. There are no right or wrong answers.

Answers

1. I have liked eating ___?___ for as long as I can remember. ....
    1. _____

2. Whenever I eat ___?___ I feel good. ......
    2. _____

3. I eat ___?___ when I am with my friends...
    3. _____

4. I eat ___?___ when I am by myself. ......
    4. _____

5. Even though it is expensive, I don't like ___?___ . ...
    5. _____

6. The most unusual food I have ever eaten was ___?___ . ...
    6. _____

7. I have never eaten ___?___ . ...
    7. _____

8. I enjoy eating ___?___ . ...
    8. _____

9. My parents wish I would eat more ___?___ .
    9. _____

10. My parents wish I would eat less ___?___ .
    10. _____

11. I eat ___?___ when I am tired or bored. ...
    11. _____

12. I like to eat ___?___ while watching television. ....
    12. _____

13. Lately, I have learned to like eating ___?___ .
    13. _____

(continued)

Answers

14. I would like to try eating ____?____ . . . .   14. _____

15. When I am really hungry I eat ____?____ . . .   15. _____

16. My favorite ethnic food is ____?____ . . . .   16. _____

17. Eating ____?____ gives me energy. . . . .   17. _____

18. If I eat too much ____?____ I feel stuffed. . . .   18. _____

19. I think I will always like to eat ____?____ . . .   19. _____

20. I think eating too much ____?____ is danger-
    ous. . . . .   20. _____

21. When I go to the movies I like to eat ____?____ .   21. _____

22. When I am in a bad mood I like to eat
    ____?____ . . . .   22. _____

23. My best friend and I often eat ____?____
    together. . . . .   23. _____

24. At parties I like to eat ____?____ . . . .   24. _____

25. I would like to learn to cook ____?____ . . . .   25. _____

26. Many of the foods we eat have ethnic, cultural, or religious origins.
    Does your family enjoy any special foods that are a part of your heritage?

    _____

    _____

    _____

27. Some foods such as steak, lobster, and caviar are expensive and taste very
    good (or at least interesting!). These foods might be called prestigious.
    Describe some foods that you would consider superior or prestigious.

    _____

    _____

    _____

    _____

    _____

LESSON 4-8

FOOD POWER

No single factor, other than heredity and training, plays as big a part in the quality of athletic performance as diet.

There are no miracle foods. Despite the fact that much good nutrition information is available, many food myths exist. The best diet (for both athletes and nonathletes) is one that supplies adequate quantities of water, calories, protein, fats, carbohydrates, minerals, and vitamins.

Athletes need to increase their water intake before, during, and after athletic events. Clothing which allows sweat to evaporate helps the body stay cool during and after exercise.

Athletes in training require a higher caloric intake than nonathletes. The increased calories should come from a variety of foods from the Basic Four Food Groups. Vitamin supplements are not needed if the food intake is balanced. Candy bars and other sugary foods will not give quick energy or added strength.

In some circumstances, certain foods and the timing of food intake may affect athletic performance. For example, researchers are trying to determine what is the best precompetition meal. It is generally agreed that the precompetition meal should be eaten three to four hours before the event so that the stomach will be relatively empty. There is some evidence that the meal should be high in carbohydrates such as cereal, bread, pasta, fruits, and vegetables because carbohydrates require the least amount of time for digestion.

1. Why is a precompetition meal of steak, French fries, and doughnuts not the best choice?

    _____

    _____

    _____

    _____

    _____

    _____

    _____

2.   Rick is going to compete in a track meet at noon.

   (a)   Write a breakfast menu below which includes carbohydrates and the Basic Four Food Groups:

   _____

   _____

   _____

   _____

   _____

   _____

   (b)   At what time should Rick eat breakfast? _____

   _____

   (c)   Rick's best friend, James, takes ten vitamin pills every morning for added strength. Should Rick do so too? _____

   (d)   At the track meet, Rick notices that members of the competing teams are eating candy bars just before competition. Why is this a bad idea?

   _____

   _____

   (e)   The competition is about to start. Rick's throat is dry and he's sweating a lot. What should he drink? _____

   (f)   Rick sets a new record during the race. After walking around to cool down, what should he drink? _____

   (g)   Next Saturday Rick has another meet. He wants to improve his performance. What should he eat in the days preceding the event?

   _____

   _____

   _____

   _____

LESSON 4-9

MENU PLANNING

Menus should always be planned to meet the nutritional
needs of the individuals to be served.

Menu planning can save time, energy, and money. The following factors
should be considered:

- The nutritional needs, likes, and dislikes of those to be served
- Money available for food
- Time, equipment, and space necessary to prepare food
- Availability of food
- Type of group to be served

The correct form for writing a menu is as follows:

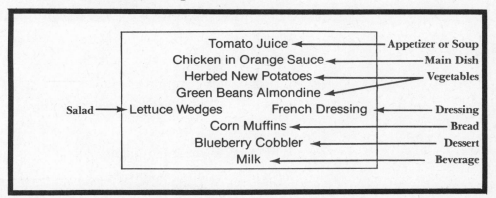

1. From the following list, circle the foods from each category you would
   pick for a dinner menu. The menu should include the Basic Four Food
   Groups and provide a variety of colors, textures, and food temperatures:

Appetizer or Soup	Main Dish	Vegetable	Salad
Chicken noodle soup	Pork chops	Yellow rice	Tossed green salad
Pineapple juice	Enchiladas	Mashed potatoes	Lime gelatin salad
Fruit cup	Roast beef	Green beans	Cole slaw
	Trout	Broccoli	
		Carrots	

Bread	Dressing or Condiments	Beverage	Dessert
Biscuits	Italian dressing	Milk	Peach ice cream
Muffins	Mayonnaise	Iced tea	Chocolate pudding
French bread	Gravy	Coffee	Cherry pie
	Poppyseed dressing	Fruit drink	Apple
	Butter	Cola	

2. Use your circled choices from the previous page and write them in correct menu form. Then answer the questions following.

_____

_____

_____

_____

_____   _____

_____

_____

_____

(a) Which foods are served hot? _____

(b) Which foods are served cool or cold? _____

(c) Which foods are crunchy or chewy? _____

(d) Which foods are smooth or soft? _____

(e) List the colors of your food choices. _____

(f) Which foods would take more than ten minutes to prepare?

_____

(g) Which foods would require more than ten minutes of waiting time (cooking or cooling) to prepare)? _____

(h) How much time would you estimate the whole meal would take to make using the equipment you have at home?

_____

(i) Could you save time by using extra pieces of equipment or by doing more than one thing at a time, such as defrosting meat in a microwave oven while cleaning vegetables at the sink?

_____

_____

(j) Review your responses and state why you would or would not change your menu choices.

_____

_____

_____

_____

_____

LESSON 4-10

FOOD SHOPPING

Food shopping is the complex process of making intelligent, informed choices from the thousands of products grocery stores offer.

Preplanning and knowledge of the marketplace aid the consumer in making the best food selections using the least amount of time and money. Consumers should remember to:

- Preshop at home: read the food ads in the newspaper, make a list, check foods and supplies on hand, clip coupons, and plan menus.

- Buy foods in season, read labels, compare prices, take advantage of advertised specials, use manufacturers' coupons, and buy only what can be used.

- Store and use foods promptly to avoid spoilage.

1. The **unit price** is the cost of a product by weight or size. Unit prices are displayed on the grocery store shelves beneath each product. Compare the two unit prices below. Which is the better buy? Product A or B?

   _____

2. Some states require that the unit price be stamped on the product as well as displayed on the shelf. Why is this a good idea from a consumer's viewpoint? _____

   _____

   _____

3.   Can the consumer tell from the unit price if one product is of better quality than another? _____

_____

The **open date** is the date stamped on products such as milk, snack foods, cereals, and cheeses which indicates when the product should be sold to ensure freshness. Products can generally be safely used two or three days after the stamped date.

4.   List products you use at home that have an open date on them:

_____   _____   _____

_____   _____   _____

_____   _____   _____

The **Universal Product Code (UPC)** is a series of black marks used for maintaining inventory, for pricing, and for identification. It can be found on the bottom or side of a package. The code can be read by automated checkout systems. The consumer cannot read the UPC unless he or she knows what the coded numbers represent.

5.   What are the advantages of the UPC for the consumer?

_____

_____

_____

_____

_____

_____

_____

_____

_____

_____

_____

LESSON 4-11

FOOD LABELS

Food labels provide useful information about the products consumers buy.

Under Food and Drug Administration (FDA) regulations, nutritional content must be listed on all food products to which a nutrient has been added or on any food for which a nutrient claim has been made. All food labels are required to include the following information:

■ Product name

■ Net weight or net contents

■ Name and place of business of the distributor, packer, and manufacturer

Even though they are not required to do so, many manufacturers include additional information such as:

■ Number of calories per serving

■ Quantity of protein, fat, carbohydrates, and sodium in a serving

■ Percentage of U.S. Recommended Daily Allowances (U.S. RDAs) of protein and seven important vitamins and minerals

■ List of ingredients (the first ingredient listed is the main ingredient in a food product; in soft drinks, the main ingredient is usually carbonated water)

1. Why would a manufacturer put more information on a food label than is required by the FDA? _____

   _____

   _____

2. (a) Name a food product of which you have read the label.

   _____

   (b) Why did you read this label? _____

   _____

   (c) Did the label contain the information you needed? _____

   _____

Sample Food Label

CLARK'S WHEAT FLAKES

**NUTRITION INFORMATION
PER SERVING**

Serving Size: 2/3 cup (1 ounce, 28.3 g)
Servings Per Box: 12

	1 oz.	with ½ cup whole milk
Calories	110	180**
Protein	3 g	7 g
Carbohydrate	23 g	29 g
Fat	Less than 1 g	4 g
Sodium	0 mg	60 mg

**PERCENTAGE OF U.S. RECOMMENDED
DAILY ALLOWANCES** (U.S. RDA)

	1 oz.	with ½ cup whole milk
Protein	4	10
Vitamin A	*	2
Vitamin C	*	*
Thiamine	4	8
Riboflavin	*	10
Niacin	8	8
Calcium	*	15
Iron	4	4
Phosphorus	10	20
Magnesium	8	10
Zinc	4	8
Copper	6	8

*Contains less than 2% of the U.S. RDA
 of these nutrients.
**Save 30 calories, use skim milk.

INGREDIENTS: 100% natural whole
wheat. To help preserve the natural
wheat flavor. BHT is added to the
packaging material.

Clark's Foods Corp.
P.O. Box 49 C
Beaumont, MS 19782

Using the information provided by the sample food label, answer the following questions:

3. How big is one serving?

   _____

4. How many servings per box are there?

   _____

5. How many additional calories does milk add?

   _____

6. What percentage of the U.S. RDA of iron is in one serving?

   _____

7. How can you save calories in using this product?

   _____

8. What is the main ingredient?

   _____

9. Is there sugar in this product?

   _____

10. Is there salt in this product?

    _____

11. Does the label have all the required information?

    _____

12. Is there BHT in this product?

    _____

UNIT 5

HEALTH AND WELLNESS: KEEPING YOURSELF FIT

UNIT 5

OBJECTIVES:

This unit provides information that will help you to:

- Develop a fitness plan
- Apply the decision-making process to decisions about alcohol, drugs, and tobacco
- Interpret peer pressure
- Identify the warning signals associated with suicide
- Recognize the symptoms of cancer
- Locate community resources that assist individuals and families with problems and crises

Keeping well and staying fit are lifelong tasks that require decision-making skill and self-discipline, but the result—feeling better about yourself—is well worth the effort. Just because you are a teenager doesn't mean that your body won't let you down. Feeling tired and lacking energy are sure signs that you are not in super shape. Concentrating on a plan that includes eating nutritious meals and exercising can help you achieve a feeling of well-being. Remember to check with your physical fitness counselor or doctor before starting any diet or exercise program.

Fitness also means making responsible decisions about the use of mood-changing drugs, alcohol, and tobacco. Finding workable alternatives through personal choice is rewarding and helps you shape a positive self-concept. Controlling the way peers influence your choices is a challenge which can help you grow and change.

People are increasingly concerned about health issues, but sometimes finding just the right source of information isn't easy. For that reason, the warning signs of suicide and the symptoms of cancer are included in this unit. The activities in this unit will help you understand why it is important to recognize the benefits of nutrition and exercise and to know the warning signs of serious health problems.

LESSON 5-1

KEEPING YOUR BODY FIT

Wellness means to keep the body and mind well and fit through a balanced daily routine of diet, exercise, and good health habits.

Complete the fitness survey below. There are no right or wrong answers.

		Never	Seldom	Often
1.	I get eight hours of sleep nearly every night.	_____	_____	_____
2.	I eat breakfast regularly.	_____	_____	_____
3.	I shower or bathe nearly every day.	_____	_____	_____
4.	I shampoo my hair more than once a week.	_____	_____	_____
5.	I go for a dental check-up twice a year.	_____	_____	_____
6.	I go to a physician when I am sick.	_____	_____	_____
7.	I have a physical at least once every two years.	_____	_____	_____
8.	I eat snack foods every day.	_____	_____	_____
9.	I try to eat nutritionally balanced meals.	_____	_____	_____
10.	I try to limit junk food in my diet.	_____	_____	_____
11.	I smoke cigarettes or use smokeless tobacco.	_____	_____	_____
12.	I drink several glasses of water per day.	_____	_____	_____
13.	I exercise every day, even if it is just walking at a fast pace.	_____	_____	_____
14.	I read the labels on food products to see what nutrients and calories I am eating.	_____	_____	_____
15.	I read the labels on all prescription and nonprescription drugs and make sure that I understand how and when the product is to be used.	_____	_____	_____

16. Which survey item would you do more often if you had the time?

_____

_____

17. Which survey item would you do more often if you had the money?

_____

_____

18. Which survey item do you do because you like doing it?

_____

_____

19. Which survey item do you do because your parents insist?

_____

_____

20. Which survey item do you consider the most important to your health? Why?

_____

_____

_____

_____

_____

21. Which survey items have become health habits?

_____

_____

_____

_____

_____

LESSON 5-2

PHYSICAL FITNESS

Physical fitness is more than being strong and looking trim. It means being in good physical condition, healthy, and able to function at your best level.

Do teenagers need to be concerned with fitness? Yes! Youth alone does not guarantee fitness. To determine if you are physically fit, you would need to be examined by a trained fitness counselor, who would evaluate the following factors:

- **Flexibility** (ease of movement)
- **Muscular strength and endurance**
- **Cardiorespiratory system** (heart and lung) endurance and efficiency
- **Body composition** (amount of fat in your body)

There are many potential **benefits** to a regular exercise program:

- Stress reduction
- Self-esteem
- Physical fitness
- Appearance (body proportions and posture)
- Energy and sense of wellness
- Companionship, if you exercise with others

There are also many **cautions** you need to be aware of before beginning an exercise program:

- Do not begin an exercise program before your physician evaluates your physical condition
- Exercise at your own rate and progress slowly
- Use proper footwear, clothing, and equipment
- Don't overeat before exercising
- Drink plenty of water
- Warm up and cool down before and after exercise
- Do not exercise vigorously in high temperatures (above 85 degrees Fahrenheit) and high humidity (above 80 percent humidity), with the exception of swimming

Fitness testing is available at most YMCAs and YWCAs and at most schools and universities. Ask your teacher about where you can get further fitness advice and instruction in your community.

1. John has joined the track team. During the first meeting with the team, the track coach plans to discuss precautions athletes should take when starting training. What sort of precautions might the coach review?

    _____

    _____

2. Aerobic exercise speeds up breathing and heart rate. Tara wants to join an aerobics class in order to improve her appearance. What other benefits might she gain?

    _____

    _____

3. Football players are often required to take ballet classes or other forms of dance training. Why would a fitness counselor suggest this?

    _____

    _____

4. Complete the following fitness log by placing an "X" in the appropriate column:

Activity	Activities You Did This Week	Activities You Plan to Do Next Week	Planned Activities Completed (fill in next week)
Walking	_____	_____	_____
Running/jogging .	_____	_____	_____
Bicycling	_____	_____	_____
Tennis	_____	_____	_____
Swimming	_____	_____	_____
Football	_____	_____	_____
Baseball	_____	_____	_____
Volleyball	_____	_____	_____
Bowling	_____	_____	_____
Basketball	_____	_____	_____
Aerobic exercise ..	_____	_____	_____
Weightlifting	_____	_____	_____
Rope skipping ...	_____	_____	_____
Rowing/sailing ...	_____	_____	_____
Dancing	_____	_____	_____
Other	_____	_____	_____

5. What activities do you need to increase? _____

LESSON 5-3

HAZARDS OF SMOKING

WARNING: The Surgeon General has determined that
cigarette smoking is dangerous to your health.

Cigarette smoking and the use of other tobacco products are harmful to
your health. Smoking is linked to lung cancer, heart disease, and respiratory ailments.

Read the statements below and check the appropriate space.

	Agree	Disagree	Don't Know
1. Most adults who smoked started smoking as teenagers.	_____	_____	_____
2. Smoking is an expensive habit.	_____	_____	_____
3. The nicotine found in cigarettes is a dependence-producing drug.	_____	_____	_____
4. Cigarette advertising often has hidden messages.	_____	_____	_____
5. There is no safe cigarette or tobacco product.	_____	_____	_____
6. Women who smoke heavily during pregnancy are more likely to miscarry or bear low–birth weight babies.	_____	_____	_____
7. On the average, 33 percent of all Americans smoke.	_____	_____	_____
8. There are equal percentages of male and female smokers in the 12 to 18 age group.	_____	_____	_____
9. Smoking one cigarette can upset the balance of air and blood in the lungs. ..	_____	_____	_____
10. The risk of lung cancer is ten times greater for smoker than for nonsmokers.	_____	_____	_____

(continued)

	Agree	Disagree	Don't Know
11. Some of the harmful effects of smoking begin to reverse themselves when the person quits smoking.	———	———	———
12. The longer a person smokes cigarettes, the more likely it is that he or she will become a heavy smoker.	———	———	———
13. Most people begin to smoke because it makes them feel grown-up or part of the crowd.	———	———	———
14. Research suggests that most teenagers don't think about the long-term effects of smoking on their health.	———	———	———
15. Nicotine is found in smokeless tobacco products and is absorbed through the lining of the mouth.	———	———	———
16. Users of smokeless tobacco suffer from a decrease in their ability to taste and smell some foods.	———	———	———
17. The heart rate and blood pressure rate increase immediately with the first puff of a cigarette.	———	———	———
18. Many cities and towns have laws and ordinances which prohibit smoking in public buildings, theaters, and restaurants.	———	———	———
19. Cigarette smoke can pollute the air in enclosed places and affects the nonsmoker.	———	———	———
20. The amount of carbon monoxide in the blood of nonsmokers doubles in a poorly ventilated room filled with cigarette smoke.	———	———	———
21. Smoke from an idling cigarette contains more tar and nicotine than an inhaled one.	———	———	———

If you agreed with all 21 statements, you are well informed about smoking. They are all true statements. If you missed one or more, you need to learn more about the harmful effects of smoking.

LESSON 5-4

BREAKING A HABIT

Thirty million Americans have quit smoking. One of the most important decisions you can make is to put your health first and not use any tobacco product.

Teenagers find that decisions about smoking are not easy. Like adults, they know they should quit, but quitting takes willpower! Many persons have successed by quitting all at once—cold turkey. Others quit by gradually smoking fewer cigarettes and substituting something pleasurable that is not harmful.

Interview a person who has quit smoking by asking them the following questions:

1. How long did you smoke? _____

2. Do you remember what made you want to smoke? _____ _____

3. Did anyone else in your family smoke? _____

4. How many cigarettes or packs did you smoke per day? _____

5. When you were smoking, were you aware of cigarette advertisements? If so, describe what type of advertising.
    _____
    _____
    _____

6. Was there anything specific about the advertisement that made you want to smoke?
    _____
    _____
    _____

7. When you started to smoke, were you aware of any health hazards associated with smoking? _____

8. Did you ever experience smoking-related health problems such as a sore throat, irritated eyes, or bronchitis? _____ If so, which one(s)? _____

9. Have you known anyone who had a smoking-related health problem? _____ . If so, which one? _____

10. Did any single event lead to your decision to stop smoking? _____ If so, what was it? _____

11. Do you agree or disagree with the legislation that protects nonsmokers from second-hand smoke? _____
    Explain your answer. _____
    _____

12. How do you feel about second-hand smoke today? _____
    _____
    _____

13. What method did you use to stop smoking? _____

14. After you quit smoking, what was the first thing you noticed about your health? _____
    _____

15. What advice would you offer an individual who wanted to stop smoking?
    _____
    _____

LESSON 5-5

PHYSIOLOGY OF SMOKING

Smoking is considered to be a factor in 325,000 deaths each year.

When a smoker lights up a cigarette or cigar, within three seconds of the very first puff the following physiological reactions begin:

- Blood pressure increases

- Heart begins to beat faster

- Carbon monoxide enters the blood

- Tar, which is composed of known **carcinogens** (cancer-causing agents) collects in the respiratory tract, disrupts the production of **mucus** (fluid secretions) and stops the action of the cilia (very small hairs that line the bronchial tubes and nose)

If you want to know how much tar is in a cigarette and what goes into the lungs when a person smokes, perform the following experiment. You will need a plastic soap bottle, a ball point pen barrel or plastic tubing, cotton, and a cigarette.

Rinse the bottle thoroughly. Make an opening in the cap to fit the tubing (pen barrel). Place the tubing into the opening and seal tightly with adhesive if necessary.

Pack cotton into the tubing. Insert a cigarette into the open end of the barrel. Press firmly on the plastic bottle to force air out before lighting the cigarette.

Slowly and regularly squeeze the bottle to simulate breathing. Withdraw the cotton from the tubing and observe the accumulation of tar.

The earlier a person begins to smoke cigarettes, the greater the risk to the smoker's health in future years. Teenagers who smoke often develop loss of stamina and signs of disease.

1.   Listed below are 24 terms associated with smoking. Using all of the words, write a newspaper article warning teenagers about the dangers of smoking. Check the glossary or a dictionary for meanings, if necessary.

atherosclerosis	cigarettes	nicotine
bad breath	cigars	odor
breathe	cilia	respiratory system
bronchitis	clothes	risk
cancer	cough	smell
carbon monoxide	emphysema	stained teeth
carcinogens	heart disease	tar
chronic condition	lung disease	tobacco

(title) _____

_____

_____

_____

_____

_____

_____

_____

_____

_____

_____

_____

_____

_____

_____

_____

_____

_____

_____

_____

_____

_____

_____

LESSON 5-6

NONSMOKERS' RIGHTS

Concern regarding the effects of secondhand smoke has
led to legislation prohibiting smoking in public places.

Nonsmokers are no longer a silent majority. Nonsmokers do care if you
smoke. Secondhand smoke pollutes the air and can have harmful effects
on nonsmokers.

1. List as many places as you can where smoking is prohibited.

    _____ _____ _____

    _____ _____ _____

    _____ _____ _____

    _____ _____ _____

    _____ _____ _____

2. Many nonsmokers feel they have a right to clean, smoke-free air. What
    can you do to protect your own nonsmokers' rights

    (a) At school? _____

    _____

    _____

    (b) At restaurants? _____

    _____

    _____

    (c) At home? _____

    _____

    _____

    (d) At work? _____

    _____

    _____

    (e) At meetings? _____

    _____

    _____

(f)   When using public transportation? _____

_____

_____

3.   Private health organizations spend millions of dollars each year spon-
soring educational programs and anti-smoking campaigns. Should tax
dollars also be spent to educate people about the hazards of smoking?
Why or why not?

_____

_____

_____

_____

_____

_____

_____

_____

_____

_____

_____

_____

_____

_____

_____

_____

_____

_____

_____

_____

LESSON 5-7

ALCOHOLISM

Teenagers have the same problems with alcohol as adults;
they are just younger.

If you think you are too young to be an alcoholic, you are wrong. No one is too young to have a problem with drinking. Alcoholism is a progressive disease characterized by compulsive drinking that is beyond the person's control. It can destroy families, wreck careers, and cause death or serious health problems, including birth defects. Alcoholics believe that drinking offers them not only an escape, but also the only satisfaction they can find in life.

Use the vocabulary words listed below to complete the essay on alcoholism. Use the glossary at the end of this book, if you don't know the meaning of a word. Use the space at the right to fill in the corresponding blank.

A.A.	community	"goofing off"	six
abusers	dependence	inhibitions	stressful
alone	depressant	judgment	susceptible
alcoholics	drink	reasoning	teenage

Answers

Alcohol is a drug which affects the nervous system. It is a (1). It will not pep you up. Instead it slows you down by controlling your (2) and thought. It interferes with your ability to perform certain mental tasks like understanding, (3), and making decisions. Alcohol also releases (4) which usually guard our behavior.

It is true that most people who drink do not become (5); however, certain properties found in alcohol are very attractive to some people who are (6) to psychological and physiological (7). These individuals may become alcoholics.

The National Institute of Alcohol Abuse and Alcoholism defines a problem (8) drinker as an individual who reports begin drunk at least (9) times a year, or experiences two or more of the following five situations during a year: trouble with teachers; trouble with family; trouble with police; driving after having a drink; or being criticized by a peer for drinking.

(continued)

1. _____

2. _____

3. _____

4. _____

5. _____

6. _____

7. _____

8. _____

9. _____

Answers

Teenagers begin to drink because they can't face up to **(10)** situations with family, friends, teachers, or employers. Signs of developing alcholism are **(11)** in school; letting grades and appearance slide; drinking **(12)**, or before school or work; and drinking to get drunk, even when you don't mean to.

10. _____

11. _____

12. _____

Teenagers should remember *before* they start to drink that

13. _____

■   Beer, a 12-ounce can, contains about the same alcohol as a shot of 86-proof whiskey or a 6-ounce glass of wine.

14. _____

■   Reaction to alcohol varies with each individual and depends upon body weight, body chemistry, the amount of food eaten, and the mood the person is in.

15. _____

■   Drinking and driving is a sure killer. Never drink and drive or accept a ride with a driver who has been drinking.

If you have a drinking problem or know of someone who does, help is available. Alcoholics Anonymous is a program to help alcoholics. Al-Anon and Alateen assist the families of alcoholics. Your **(13)** may have an **(14)** program or other programs specifically designed for alcohol **(15)**.

16.   Find these resources and phone numbers in your telephone directory and write them below.

_____

_____

_____

_____

_____

_____

_____

_____

_____

_____

_____

_____

_____

_____

_____

_____

LESSON 5-8

SELF-AWARENESS AND DRUG USE

Feelings about self are related to behavior and decision-making about drug use.

A negative perception of oneself is a major factor in the development of drug-abusing habits. It is important to learn how to feel good about yourself. One way to feel good is to give yourself positive messages by finding those personal qualities within yourself that are self-esteem "builders."

Check your responses to the following self-awareness checklist:

		Yes	No	Sometimes
1.	I am honest with myself and others. .	_____	_____	_____
2.	I am a good conversationalist.	_____	_____	_____
3.	I am enthusiastic about life.	_____	_____	_____
4.	I am sincere and warm with others. . .	_____	_____	_____
5.	I use my time wisely.	_____	_____	_____
6.	I plan the use of money.	_____	_____	_____
7.	I have a sense of humor.	_____	_____	_____
8.	I am patient and understanding.	_____	_____	_____
9.	I have a loving and supporting home life.	_____	_____	_____
10.	I am planning my future career.	_____	_____	_____
11.	I practice good health habits.	_____	_____	_____
12.	I like the way I look.	_____	_____	_____
13.	I am skilled in sports.	_____	_____	_____
14.	I am talented in music or art.	_____	_____	_____
15.	I try to collect all the information I need to help solve my problems.	_____	_____	_____
16.	I complete projects I start.	_____	_____	_____
17.	I try to learn from my mistakes.	_____	_____	_____

(continued)

	Yes	No	Sometimes

18. I have a lot of energy and enjoy
     being active. . . . .   _____   _____   _____

19. I enjoy participating in school and
     community activities. . . . .   _____   _____   _____

20. I am motivated to do well in school. .   _____   _____   _____

21. Improving your self-esteem begins by knowing that it can be better.
     Choose one self-esteem builder from your list which needs improvement
     and design a self-improvement plan.

22. The one area where I need to improve is _____ .

23. What resources (human and material) might you use in your self-
     improvement plan?

     _____   _____   _____

     _____   _____   _____

     _____   _____   _____

24. Which alternatives will you consider?

     _____   _____   _____

25. Which alternative will you choose? _____

26. How will you take action on your choice? _____

     _____

27. How will you evaluate your plan? _____

     _____

     _____

     _____

LESSON 5-9

DECISION-MAKING AND DRUGS

The best defenses against substance abuse are positive
self-esteem and the ability to make good decisions.

Use the vocabulary words listed below to complete the essay on substance
abuse. If you do not know the meaning of one of the words in the list,
use the glossary at the end of this book. Use the space at the right to fill in
the corresponding blank.

aerosol	culture	experiment	hooked	overdosed	sniffing
alcohol	death	grass	LSD	pep pills	sober
cannabis	dependent	habit	nauseous	pot	stimulant
cocaine	drug	hallucinations	no	self-esteem	substance

Answers

This is the story of Jake the Junkie. He was a fellow who didn't
think very much of himself. He had low **(1)**. He also had a habit of
making bad decisions. He thought he knew a lot about drugs, but he
didn't. He didn't know that any substance that enters the body and has
an effect on the mind or body is called a **(2)**.

Jake started down the road to **(3)** abuse when he started building
model airplanes and began **(4)** the glue. He didn't know that inhaling
an **(5)** or solvent could actually cause **(6)**. When a friend gave him
some **(7)** he didn't know they were amphetamines, a **(8)**. Jake could
have said **(9)**, but he didn't because he didn't want to appear afraid or
"chicken." Do you know what happened to Jake? He ended up in the
hospital. The doctor said he was having **(10)**.

After the experience, Jake said "Never again," but then he was
invited to a party where there was **(11)**. He thought to himself, "Everyone is trying it so it can't be that bad." After all, he wanted to be
accepted. He began to slur his speech, and the next thing he knew he
was very **(12)**. Luckily for Jake, a **(13)** friend offered to drive him home.

The next day, a teacher was telling the class about the dangers of
marijuana, a drug often referred to by its slang name, **(14)**. It comes
from a drug family called **(15)**, but Jake wasn't interested in listening
to any more lectures on marijuana. He has been smoking **(16)** for a
long time. In fact, he has concluded that he was **(17)** or **(18)** on it.

1. _____
2. _____
3. _____
4. _____
5. _____
6. _____
7. _____
8. _____
9. _____
10. _____
11. _____
12. _____
13. _____
14. _____
15. _____
16. _____
17. _____
18. _____

(continued)

Answers

To make a long story short, Jake began to **(19)** with other drugs including **(20)** and **(21)**. He drifted into a drug **(22)** to support his **(23)**. The last anyone heard about Jake was that he had **(24)**.

19. _____

20. _____

21. _____

22. _____

23. _____

24. _____

25. What decisions did Jake make that led him to substance abuse?

_____

_____

_____

_____

_____

_____

26. Taking an **alternative** is choosing to do something else. What alternatives could you have suggested for Jake?

_____

_____

_____

_____

_____

_____

LESSON 5-10

SAYING NO TO DRUGS

Teenagers often are pressured by peers to try drugs. Learning to say no means standing up for your own rights, values, and beliefs.

Has anyone ever asked you to do something you really didn't want to do? Going against your better judgment and yielding to peer influence is yielding to **peer pressure**. Saying no to peer pressure requires a "think-fast response." The trick is to develop quick responses using humor and courage. Saying no is not easy, but it is a skill that improves with practice. Here are some pointers:

- Say no and keep repeating it in one form or another.

- Say no and then change the focus of the discussion to something you are interested in.

- Say no and be consistent by stating your reasons.

- Say no and be firm by making it clear that you are not going to change your mind.

- Say no and then think to yourself, "If I say yes, another person will be influencing my life by disregarding my rights, values, and beliefs."

- Say no and remember that it may be better to be alone than to be influenced by another.

1. A friend asks you to meet after school to smoke some "pot." You have decided that you are not interested in trying marijuana, but you are afraid you will lose a friend if you say no. Choose three of the suggestions from the above list and describe how you would tell your friend no.

   (a) _____

   _____

   _____

   _____

   _____

   _____

   _____

(b) _____

_____

_____

_____

_____

_____

_____

(c) _____

_____

_____

_____

_____

_____

_____

2.   Describe an experience when you did yield to peer pressure. How did you feel after the experience? What made you say yes when you really wanted to say no?

_____

_____

_____

_____

_____

_____

_____

_____

_____

_____

_____

_____

_____

_____

_____

_____

_____

LESSON 5-11

SUICIDE WARNING SIGNALS

Suicide is the intentional killing of oneself. The teenage suicide rate has more than tripled in the past 20 years; it is the second leading cause of death among persons aged 10 to 24 years.

Suicide is a tragic event. In the United States, 5,000 young people committed suicide last year. It is estimated that 75 percent of suicides are preceded by certain recognizable behaviors or warning signals. Even one of these warning signs is an emergency. It means you must get help right away for yourself or the person in danger.

The following is a list of warning signals:

- A significant decline in school grades and performance
- A significant change in eating or sleeping habits or both
- Giving away of prized possessions
- Neglect of personal appearance
- Breakdown in relationships between parents, siblings, peers, boyfriend, or girlfriend
- Feeling tired all the time without being sick
- Withdrawal from normal activities and friends
- A long depression over the loss of a loved one
- Feeling constantly restless or frantic overactivity
- Feelings of self-hate, worthlessness, or discouragement
- Inability to enjoy self and express pleasure
- Involvement with drugs or alcohol or both
- Truancy, running away, or accident proneness
- Unwillingness or inability to communicate with others
- Behaviors which are inconsistent with previous patterns
- Suicidal thoughts
- A suicide attempt

The most important thing to remember is that if someone close to you is talking or even hinting about suicide, do not ignore the message. People who talk about suicide usually attempt suicide, and many are successful. Here are some tips to follow:

■   Be supportive and communicate that you care.

■   Encourage the person to talk to others and to seek professional help.

■   Be a good listener. Be sympathetic, but do not give false hope by saying, "Everything will work out for the best."

■   Believe that the person is capable of suicide. Never ignore a suicide threat.

■   Never dare or challenge a person to commit suicide.

■   Use your own good judgment. Go to a trusted teacher, parent, counselor, minister, priest, or rabbi for help.

■   Help the person find community resources; for example, look up phone numbers and addresses of mental health organizations or community services.

■   Stress that death cannot be reversed.

In an emergency:

■   Do not leave the person alone, but contact an adult as soon as possible.

■   Call police or emergency 911.

■   Call the suicide hot line (listed in the telephone book).

■   Call hospital emergency.

■   Call the telephone operator and ask for help.

■   Call a local community health center.

What resources are available to persons considering suicide in your community?

_____

_____

_____

_____

_____

_____

_____

_____

_____

_____

_____

LESSON 5-12

BREAST AND TESTICULAR SELF-EXAMINATION FOR CANCER PREVENTION

One out of every 11 women will get breast cancer at some point during her lifetime.

Breast self-examination should be done once a month, one week following menstruation. Any lump or thickening in the breast or surrounding area should be examined by a doctor immediately. If a malignant breast lump is found while it is still small and before it has spread, one's chances of survival are excellent.

To perform breast self-examination,* follow these steps:

1. Looking in the mirror, put your arms at your sides. Do your breasts look the same as they usually do? Remember that many women normally have one breast that is smaller than the other. It's important to know what is normal for you.

2. Still looking in the mirror, put your arms up. Look for any changes in contour of each breast (a swelling, dimpling of skin, or changes in the nipple).

3. Lie flat. Put a pillow or folded towel under your left shoulder. Put your left hand under your head. Use your right hand, fingers flattened, to check your left breast.

4. Work in a spiral, from the outside edge of your breast in toward the nipple. You'll probably feel a firm ridge around the lower edge of your breast. That's normal.

5. Now change for the right breast. Put the pillow under your right shoulder with your right arm under your head. Slowly repeat the examination.

*Courtesy of the American Cancer Society (adapted).

A recent survey by the National Institute of Cancer shows that 46 percent of all Americans incorrectly believe that nothing can be done to prevent cancer. Physicians and medical researchers do not agree on the causes of cancer, but they generally agree that good health habits form the foundation of a life plan which can help prevent cancer. These health habits include the following suggestions (adapted from the American Cancer Society):

■ Take care of yourself by eating a balanced diet low in fat and high in fiber and vitamins A and C—for example, broccoli, beans, seeds, spinach, potatoes, cereals, and grains.

■ Exercise regularly.

■ Don't smoke or use smokeless tobacco products.

■ Avoid excessive use of alcohol.

■ Avoid excessive exposure to the sun (especially between the hours of 11 A.M. and 2 P.M.).

■ Avoid unnecessary x-rays.

■ Avoid excessive exposure to chemicals.

■ Know the seven warning signs of cancer: **(1)** change in bowel or bladder habits, **(2)** a sore that does not heal, **(3)** unusual bleeding or discharge, **(4)** thickening or lump in breast or elsewhere, **(5)** indigestion or difficulty in swallowing, **(6)** obvious change in wart or mole, **(7)** nagging cough or hoarseness.

One of the most common cancers in young men is cancer of the **testes**, the male reproductive glands. It can be treated effectively if discovered early. Symptoms of testicular cancer include a slight enlargement of one of the testes, a change in its consistency, or a dull pain in the lower abdomen and groin. Self-examination is important. Each month, take a few minutes to roll each testicle gently between the thumb and fingers of both hands. If you discover any hard lumps or nodules, it is important that you see a doctor immediately.

LESSON 5-13

FINDING HELP

When an individual or family has a problem too tough to solve alone, it is important to know where to find help.

Locating specific community resources and information can be troublesome. Check the following sources first:

- Telephone directory (White Pages under "Health," "Social Services," "Mental Health," and "County/City Welfare Departments," Yellow Pages under "Social Services")

- Telephone counseling and referral services

- Community services directory

- Law enforcement agencies

- School counselors and teachers

- Private physicians and hospitals

- Legal aid society

- Local health department

- Private agencies—for example, the American Cancer Society

- Churches and synagogues

- Public libraries

- Consumer affairs departments

- Colleges and universities (some offer free or low-cost counseling services)

Locate sources, addresses, and phone numbers in your community for individuals and families with the following concerns:

Problem	Agency/Phone #	Cost of Services
1. Tenant/landlord disputes . .		
2. Drug abuse		
3. Cancer information		
4. Truancy		
5. Pregnancy/VD		
6. Alcohol abuse		
7. Child abuse		
8. Money problems		
9. Suicide		
10. Marital problems		
11. Runaways		
12. Rape		
13. Smoking information		
14. Depression		
15. Child support enforcement .		

UNIT 6

COMMUNICATION: YOU AND OTHERS

UNIT 6

OBJECTIVES:

This unit provides information that will help you to:

- Understand the dynamics of effective communication
- Develop speaking and listening skills
- Describe forms of verbal and nonverbal communication
- Recognize that a positive self-concept influences effective communication skills
- Distinguish between positive and negative conflict resolution

Have you ever stopped to think about how many hours you spend each day communicating? It is estimated that the average person spends approximately 75 percent of his or her waking hours in some form of communication. **Communication** is the process of transmitting a message from a sender to a receiver. It sounds simple, but if everyone communicated more effectively there would be fewer arguments, conflicts, and misunderstandings. There would be more peace in families and harmony between friends.

Communication is basic to all human relationships. Since the adolescent years represent a period when meaningful relationships are established, it is a crucial time for building communication skills. The way you communicate with others can say a lot about how you view yourself. One of the best ways to feel good about yourself is to help others feel good about themselves; and if you want to get along with others, you have to communicate with them. You can improve your communication skills by being open and honest. When conflicts arise, be reasonable and work at finding constructive solutions. Always consider the other person's point of view and say what you mean. Remember, everything you say and do is a form of communication. The lessons in this unit will help you understand how you communicate and will give you an opportunity to practice communication skills with others.

LESSON 6-1

COMMUNICATION STYLES

Communication styles reveal one's self-concept, opinions, and feelings.

Your communication style is generally very close to your personality. Young adults who communicate well gain respect among their peers and often become leaders in their schools and communities.

Assertive communication is what you use to express your rights, opinions, needs, and feelings. It is straightforward and direct, and it doesn't put other people down. Sharing, closeness, fairness, and growth are characteristics of effective assertive communication.

Nonassertive communication is a failure to express your rights, opinions, needs, and feelings. This approach is vague and indirect. Conflict is usually avoided, but the individual pays a price in terms of lower self-esteem, unmet needs, and increased conflict in the future.

Aggressive communication denies the rights, resources, or dignity of another person. This method usually makes others angry and then all positive communication breaks down.

This lesson will help you become more aware of your communication style.

1. Describe your primary style of communication with others.

    _____

    _____

    _____

    _____

2. Your best friend asks you to go to a party. Tell your friend in assertive language that you don't want to go.

    _____

    _____

    _____

    _____

3. Describe how you would tell a friend in nonassertive language that you don't want to go to a party.

_____

_____

_____

_____

4. It is often easier to be assertive with some people and nonassertive or aggressive with others.

   (a) I find it difficult to be assertive with _____

   (b) I am always assertive with _____

   (c) I would describe my communication style with my parent(s) as

   _____ because I _____

   _____

   (d) I would describe my communication style with my best friend as

   _____ because I _____

   _____

   (e) I would describe my communication style with strangers as _____

   _____ because I _____

   _____

   (f) I would describe my communication style with my teachers as

   _____ because I _____

   _____

   (g) I would describe my communication style with my peers as _____

   _____ because I _____

   _____

5. How would you change your communication style? _____

_____

_____

_____

_____

_____

_____

_____

_____

LESSON 6-2

SELF-CONCEPT AND COMMUNICATION

Communication is important in creating an environment
that helps us feel good about ourselves and others.

One of the best ways to build a positive environment for communication is
to let others know that they are OK, that you feel good about them. If
you help others feel good about themselves, you will feel good too, and everyone will have a better self-concept.

1.   List ten adjectives or phrases that could be used in helping others feel
     good about themselves.

     1. _____   6. _____

     2. _____   7. _____

     3. _____   8. _____

     4. _____   9. _____

     5. _____   10. _____

2.   Write two things you would like to communicate to your parent(s) that
     would make them feel good about themselves.

     _____

     _____

3.   Describe two things you would like to communicate to a brother or
     sister that would make them feel good about themselves.

     _____

     _____

4.   Write two things you would like to communicate to a teacher that would
     make him or her feel good about himself or herself.

     _____

     _____

5.   Write two things you would like to communicate to a special friend that would make him or her feel good about himself or herself.

_____

_____

6.   Has someone said something to you recently that made you feel good about yourself?

(a)   Who said it? _____

(b)   What did they say? _____

_____

(c)   How did you respond? _____

_____

_____

(d)   How did you feel about what they said? _____

_____

_____

7.   Some people have difficulty accepting praise or compliments. Why does this happen? _____

_____

_____

8.   Write two things you would like to communicate to yourself that will make you feel good about yourself.

_____

_____

LESSON 6-3

VERBAL AND NONVERBAL COMMUNICATION

Communication is a two-way process involving sharing and understanding between two or more people.

Communication is the complex process of sending (or speaking) and receiving (listening) verbal and nonverbal messages. Effective communication can exist only when the receiver interprets the sender's message in the same way the speaker intended it.

To be a good sender you must know what you want to say and then say it. It is important to make eye contact with the receiver. Look for clues such as facial expressions that let you know the receiver is getting the message you are sending.

To be a good receiver you must make eye contact with the sender. Look for nonverbal clues such as gestures and tone of voice to help you interpret what the speaker is saying before you respond.

1. This lesson will help you become more aware of how you communicate with others. Describe how you would communicate the following feelings *verbally*. If possible, practice with someone you know.

    (a) Frustration _____

    _____

    (b) Anger _____

    _____

    (c) Grief _____

    _____

    (d) Envy _____

    _____

    (e) Pride _____

    _____

2. Describe how you would communicate the following emotions *non-verbally*. If possible, practice with someone you know.

   (a) Fear _____

   _____

   (b) Love _____

   _____

   (c) Aggression _____

   _____

   (d) Depression _____

   _____

   (e) Joy _____

   _____

3. Cite an example of how nonverbal communication takes place between:

   (a) Parent and child _____

   _____

   (b) Brother and sister _____

   _____

   (c) Teacher and student _____

   _____

   (d) Employer and employee _____

   _____

LESSON 6-4

SENDING SKILLS

Sending involves saying what one means to say, with agreement between verbal and nonverbal messages.

A responsible sender talks *with* people, not *at* them, and considers the listener's feelings and opinions. What kind of sender are you?

	Always	Sometimes	Never
1. I try to send messages that are clear and specific.	_____	_____	_____
2. I ask for feedback.	_____	_____	_____
3. My verbal and nonverbal messages are the same.	_____	_____	_____
4. I look at people when I speak.	_____	_____	_____
5. I try to be aware of the other person's point of view.	_____	_____	_____
6. I try to avoid blaming and preaching in my messages.	_____	_____	_____
7. I find it hard to talk in front of other people.	_____	_____	_____
8. I raise my voice instead of making my point stronger.	_____	_____	_____
9. I argue instead of discussing differences of opinion.	_____	_____	_____
10. I use polite phrases when making requests.	_____	_____	_____
11. I avoid speech mannerisms such as "you know."	_____	_____	_____

12. Review your responses. How could you improve your sending skills?

_____

_____

_____

_____

_____

13. What might you do and how might you feel if the person you were speaking with:

    (a) Started talking to someone else _____

    _____

    (b) Became silent and acted disinterested _____

    _____

    (c) Gave advice you didn't want _____

    _____

    (d) Misinterpreted what you said _____

    _____

    (e) Started to "cut you down" _____

    _____

    (f) Began to gossip about your best friend _____

    _____

14. Cite an example of a time when a sender talked *at* you and not *with* you.

    _____

    _____

    _____

    _____

    _____

LESSON 6-5

LISTENING SKILLS

Listening involves hearing what is said and observing the actions communicated.

A responsible listener attempts to tell the speaker how the message is being received, or asks questions for clarification. What kind of listener are you?

		Always	Sometimes	Never
1.	I accept what is being said just because of who is saying it.	_____	_____	_____
2.	I listen more for facts than ideas.	_____	_____	_____
3.	I feel angry and frustrated when someone tells me about my faults. ...	_____	_____	_____
4.	I am easily distracted by sights and sounds.	_____	_____	_____
5.	I tend to "tune out" things I don't want to hear.	_____	_____	_____
6.	I tend to judge others by how they communicate.	_____	_____	_____
7.	I try to concentrate on what the speaker is saying.	_____	_____	_____
8.	I try to look at people when they speak.	_____	_____	_____
9.	I try to recognize the speaker's purpose.	_____	_____	_____
10.	I look for nonverbal clues that will help me interpret what the speaker is saying.	_____	_____	_____
11.	I try to respond appropriately.	_____	_____	_____
12.	I don't like to hear negative comments about myself.	_____	_____	_____

13.   Review your responses. How could you improve your listening skills?

_____

_____

_____

_____

_____

_____

14.   What is meant by the statement, "Listen with your eyes"?

_____

_____

_____

_____

_____

_____

15.   One way to show someone you are interested in what they have to say is to ask questions. What types of questions could you ask another person to get to know them better?

_____

_____

_____

_____

_____

_____

16.   To empathize means to be sensitive to another person's feelings, situation, and concerns. Cite an example of how you empathize with others.

_____

_____

_____

_____

_____

_____

_____

_____

_____

LESSON 6-6

"I" MESSAGES AND "YOU" MESSAGES

"I" Messages are simple statements of fact about how you feel or think. **"You" Messages** are statements that ascribe blame or judge others and promote arguments.

Consider "I" Messages and "You" Messages in responding to the following communications. Beneath each statement write (**a**) an "I" Message and (**b**) a "You" Message.

Example: Your mother says, "If you are going to be part of this household you are going to have to clean up your room."

(**a**) *I admit I am lazy when it comes to cleaning up my room. I am going to try to improve.*

(**b**) *All you do is complain. My room is just fine. If it bothers you so much I'll keep the door shut and you stay out.*

1. Your dad says, "If you tease your sister once more you are grounded for a month."

    (**a**) _____

    _____

    (**b**) _____

    _____

2. Your boyfriend says, "You've broken our last three dates. What's the matter—don't you want to go out with me any more?"

    (**a**) _____

    _____

    (**b**) _____

    _____

3. Your girlfriend says, "Your driving has gone from bad to worse. Are you trying to get us killed?"

   (a) _____

       _____

   (b) _____

       _____

4. A teacher says, "You haven't been paying attention, and your grades are going down because of it."

   (a) _____

       _____

   (b) _____

       _____

5. Your employer says, "You can't be late for work and expect me to treat you the same as my employees who are on time."

   (a) _____

       _____

   (b) _____

       _____

6. Your brother says, "You promised that you would drive me to town and now you say you are too tired."

   (a) _____

       _____

   (b) _____

       _____

7. Why is an "I" Message more effective than a "You" Message?

_____

_____

_____

_____

LESSON 6-7

COMMUNICATING WITH PARENTS

Communicating means to express yourself so another person can understand what you are thinking and feeling.

Knowing things about how your parents grew up may help you better understand and communicate with them now. This lesson will give you the opportunity to interview your parents.

1. What did you enjoy discussing with your parents when you were a teenager?

    _____

    _____

    _____

    _____

2. Did your parents agree on how to discipline children?

    _____

    _____

    _____

    _____

3. What is the happiest memory you have of your childhood?

    _____

    _____

    _____

    _____

4. What is the saddest memory you have of your childhood?

    _____

    _____

    _____

    _____

5. Did your parents discuss the pros, cons, and alternatives of things you wanted to do?

_____

_____

_____

6. When you were growing up, who planned the family activities?

_____

_____

_____

7. What were holidays like in your family when you were growing up?

_____

_____

_____

8. What are some family customs or traditions that have been passed down to our family today?

_____

_____

_____

9. Did you communicate equally well with both parents?

_____

_____

_____

_____

10. If you could change something about communicating with your own parents, what would it be?

_____

_____

_____

_____

11. What are some of the key points you learned from giving your parents this survey?

_____

_____

_____

_____

LESSON 6-8

RESOLVING CONFLICT

Interpersonal conflicts exist whenever an action by one person interferes in some way with the actions of another.

Constructive conflicts focus on the issue or problem. They often result in your knowing people better, developing better listening skills, strengthening your relationships, and bringing issues out into the open.

Destructive conflicts involve attacks on the person. They often result in break-ups of friendships, attacks on self-esteem, instances of yelling, screaming, or abuse, and extension of the conflict beyond the original issue.

Read the following case study and resolve the conflict using **(a)** constructive resolution and **(b)** destructive resolution.

1. Amy and Georgia were working together on a school project. One night as they worked together Amy's boyfriend came by and asked her to go with him on a quick errand. Amy agreed, leaving Georgia to work on the project alone. Amy returned two hours later. Georgia then told her that if she had known she was going to be gone for two hours she . . .

   (a) _____

   _____

   _____

   _____

   _____

   _____

   _____

   (b) _____

   _____

   _____

   _____

   _____

   _____

   _____

2.   Describe an interpersonal conflict you experienced which was resolved *constructively*. Use fictional names.

_____

_____

_____

_____

_____

_____

_____

_____

_____

_____

3.   Describe an interpersonal conflict you experienced which was resolved *destructively*. Use fictional names.

_____

_____

_____

_____

_____

_____

_____

_____

_____

_____

4.   Describe what you have learned from these experiences.

_____

_____

_____

_____

_____

_____

_____

_____

_____

LESSON 6-9

DEFENDING YOUR POINT OF VIEW

It is sometimes necessary to have an argument to resolve
points of difference, clear the air, or relieve tension.

Learning to defend your point of view can help you feel better about yourself and help you communicate more effectively.

Respond to the following statements:

1. How do you know when an issue or problem is worth arguing about?

    _____

    _____

    _____

    _____

2. Do you listen to the other person's point of view before responding?

    _____

    _____

    _____

3. What are the costs and benefits of trying to avoid arguments?

    _____

    _____

    _____

4. Why is it important to defend your point of view even if no one else
    agrees with you?

    _____

    _____

    _____

    _____

5.   If you find yourself in a situation where you must defend your point of view, what methods do you use? That is, do you speak and listen calmly, yell at your opponent, walk away, shift blame, or pout? Cite an example of an argument you had recently and the method you used.

_____

_____

_____

_____

_____

_____

_____

_____

_____

_____

6.   How would you handle the following situations without becoming involved in an argument?

(a)   You catch your best friend in a lie.

_____

_____

_____

_____

_____

(b)   Your parents have asked you to babysit but you have made other plans.

_____

_____

_____

_____

_____

(c)   You are offered a ride home, but you don't want to accept because you know the driver has a bad driving record.

_____

_____

_____

_____

_____

UNIT 7

COMMUNITY: YOU AND A JOB

UNIT 7

OBJECTIVES:

This unit provides information that will help you to:

- Locate job openings
- Complete a job application form
- Write a letter of application
- Develop a résumé
- Apply for a Social Security card
- Understand a W-2 tax form

Goals you set about your future occupation or career are among the most important decisions you will ever make. Unfortunately, many high school students do not have realistic career goals or expectations. They simply do not know how to plan or how to get started. Many others lack the self-discipline, motivation, and other personal qualities necessary to find and keep a job.

Most careers begin with a first job. High school students seek jobs for a number of reasons, including earning money and gaining experience. The temporary, part-time jobs that attract teenagers offer the opportunity of testing work preferences, skills, and abilities before making long-term commitments. This period of personal inventory is an important first step. Think about the things you enjoy doing, your hobbies and interests, and unpaid jobs you have done for others that have given you satisfaction. Use these as a guide in looking for a job opening. Step two is to set a goal and write it down. Begin to map your future, considering all the options that are open to you: continuing your education, getting vocational training, staying with the job you have but looking for advancement, or combining more education and a job. The lessons in this unit will help you plan for your first job. Good luck!

LESSON 7-1

READING HELP-WANTED ADS

Locating job openings is the first step in finding a job.

The serious job seeker explores many sources of job information:

- Help-wanted advertisements in newspapers
- Word of mouth—friends and relatives may know of jobs
- Help-wanted signs in store windows
- Private employment agencies (which charge a fee)
- Public employment agencies (which offer free services)
- Direct contact with employers by phone or mail or in person

Read the classified advertisements below and answer the questions following.

CASHIERS

Self-service gas station. Clean, inside work. Good starting pay with regular increases. Must be honest, neat, and reliable. Jack's Service Station, 850 11th Ave.

GREAT STUDENT JOB

Food prep. and general kitchen work. Mon.-Fri. flexible hours. Come by The Eatery and see Mr. Marsh for interview. 711 8th Ave.

MOTHER'S HELPER

Love of children a must. After school until 6 P.M. Only responsible, dependable, caring individuals need apply. 878-6329.

PART-TIME RETAIL SALES
HOURLY WAGE AND COMMISSION

I need a few enthusiastic, smiling people who enjoy meeting and greeting customers at large local department store. The applicant should be sports minded and possess a high energy level. Call Miss Atkins, 385-9377, between 9 A.M. and 3 P.M. for interview.

1.   Which advertisement would you be most likely to answer? _____
_____

2.   What personal qualities is the employer looking for? _____
_____

3.   What education or training have you had that would help you get this
job? _____
_____

4.   What are the job tasks, duties, or expectations? _____
_____

5.   What hourly salary do you think this job pays? _____

6.   If the employer tells you that the job pays the minimum wage, how
much will you receive per hour? _____

7.   In the space below write an advertisement for a job you would like to
apply for. Include duties, personal qualities, and wages.

_____

_____

_____

_____

_____

_____

_____

_____

_____

_____

_____

_____

_____

_____

_____

_____

_____

LESSON 7-2

JOB APPLICATIONS

Completing a job application is an important step in getting a job.

A job application form gives the employer personal information about you as well as an idea about how you express yourself and about your ability to follow directions. A job application form is the employer's first look at who you are. It is important to give a good first impression.

In completing a job application form:

- Follow all directions exactly as they are written.

- Be neat and clear, and avoid careless mistakes.

- Use black or blue ink (always carry a pen with you).

- Complete all questions that apply. If a question does not apply, write "not applicable" or "N/A."

- Be accurate about your employment and education experience. If necessary, carry this information with you.

- Know your Social Security number.

- If references are requested, give accurate names, addresses, and phone numbers. Be certain the people you list as references will speak highly of you.

- Know which job you are applying for and what salary you want.

- If a job requires a license or certificate, have a copy of it with you.

1. Complete the job application form below using information about yourself.

APPLICATION FOR EMPLOYMENT

Name _____ Date _____

Address _____

Phone No. _____ Social Security No. _____

Position Desired _____ Salary Desired _____

Education	Name and Address	Dates Attended		Date Graduated	Major Area of Study
		From	To		
High School					
Vocational School					
Other					

Courses taken in school which will assist you with this job: _____

_____

Employment: List most recent employer first. Use extra sheet if necessary.

Name and Address of Employer	Dates Employed		Position	Reason for Leaving
	From	To		

References: Do not list relatives.

Name	Address	Telephone	How Long Known

Are you currently employed? _____ Date available for work _____

LESSON 7-3

LETTER OF APPLICATION

A letter of application is a way of "selling" yourself to a prospective employer.

Writing a good letter of application is an important skill. It should reflect your personality and show the employer that you are a solid, sincere, dependable person. A good letter of application should:

- Be typewritten or written on unlined paper using blue or black ink
- Be neat and free of errors
- Be as brief as possible, but state the exact job you want
- State your education and training
- State your past experience and one reference
- Let the employer know that you would like an interview and where you can be reached

```
                                        1001 S. Meridian Place
                                        Chicago, IL  30987-2419
                                        September 19, 1986


Mr. Thomas A. Sharp
Personnel Director
ABC Computer Corp.
6789 West Ave.
Chicago, IL  30987-2481


Dear Mr. Sharp:

Your recent ad in the Times Record for computer repair trainees was of interest to me.
I am enclosing my resume outlining my qualifications for the position.

I have completed several computer courses at the Regional Vocational Center, including Data
Processing, Beginning and Advanced Programming, and Keypunch.  I am working in computer
sales, but would like to acquire computer service skills.  My employer, Mrs. Jane Bloom
of Computer City, will confirm that I have the initiative, skills, and personal traits to
become a contributing member of your staff.

I would appreciate the opportunity to meet with you to explore our mutual interests and
to provide you with any additional information you may need.  You can contact me at my home
phone, (312) 555-0110, after 4 P.M.

Thank you for your consideration.

Sincerely,

Todd Learner

Todd Learner
```

Write your own letter of application below.

_____

_____

_____

_____

_____

_____

_____

_____

_____

_____

_____

_____

_____

_____

_____

_____

_____

_____

_____

LESSON 7-4

WRITING A RÉSUMÉ

A résumé is a summary of your previous work experience, education, and other job qualifications.

A good résumé should:

- Be typewritten or written on unlined paper with blue or black ink
- Be neat and free of errors
- Be accurate and well organized
- State your past work experience and education
- State one or more professional and personal references
- Be accompanied by a letter of application if mailed to the potential employer

---

Sample Resume

```
Todd Learner
1001 S. Meridian Place
Chicago, IL  30987-2419
(312) 555-0110

Employment Objective
Computer Repair Trainee          I feel that I am qualified for this position because
                                 of my previous work experience, my vocational training
                                 in the computer field, and my ability to meet the public.


Education
September 1981 - June 1985       Lakeside High School
                                 Chicago, IL  30987-2411
                                 Diploma granted/Completed general studies track

July 1985 to present             Enrolled in Regional Vocational Center studying Computer
                                 Science.

Work Experience
June 1985 to present             Computer City, Sales
                                 3330 Central Ave.
                                 Chicago, IL  30987-2099

Interests                        Tennis, swimming and meeting people

References                       Available upon request
```

In the space below, create a résumé using information about yourself.

RÉSUMÉ

Employment Objective

Education

Work Experience

Interests

References

LESSON 7-5

APPLYING FOR A SOCIAL SECURITY CARD

Your **Social Security card number** is the way the government keeps a correct record of your earnings when you are employed. The number is also needed if you die, retire, or become disabled so that you or your survivors can receive benefits.

Before making application for a Social Security card you must have documented evidence of who you are. You will need:

- Evidence of your age (Your birth certificate is the preferred document. Religious records of birth or baptism or a hospital record of birth can also be used in some circumstances.)

- Evidence of identity (You can use school ID card, report card, driver's license, vaccination certificate, insurance policy, or voter's registration card.)

- Evidence of U.S. citizenship or lawful alien status

Legal guardians or legal custodians can apply for a Social Security card for a child by providing evidence of the child's age and citizenship and evidence of their own identity.

You may apply for a Social Security card either by mailing your documents of evidence and application form to the nearest Social Security office or by going to the office in person. You must apply in person if:

- You are 18 or older and have never had a Social Security number before.

- You are an alien whose immigration documents should not be mailed.

All questions about Social Security numbers and your record of earnings should be directed to your local Social Security office (listed under "U.S. Government" in the telephone book).

The front of your Social Security card will indicate your number and your name. You should sign your name on the signature line. Note the way Social Security numbers are written: 000-00-0000. Always write your number exactly as it appears on your card. The back of the card has important information regarding when you should contact the Social Security office.

Social Security Card

Front   Back

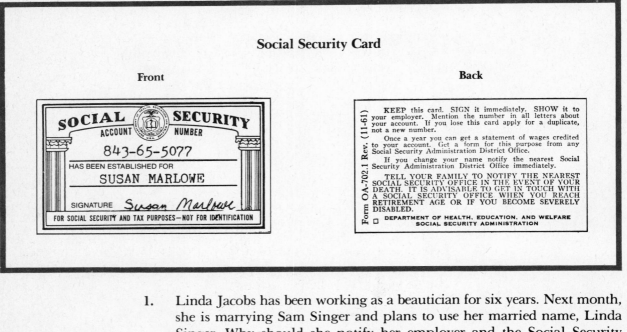

1. Linda Jacobs has been working as a beautician for six years. Next month, she is marrying Sam Singer and plans to use her married name, Linda Singer. Why should she notify her employer and the Social Security office about her name change?

   _____

   _____

   _____

2. Stephanie is 16 and wants to get a job as a waitress. A local restaurant manager says that he cannot hire her until he has a copy of her Social Security card. Why does the manager have to see her Social Security card?

   _____

   _____

   _____

3. Bill Walters wants a Social Security number for his three-year-old son. Can he get one? _____ Why would a parent want a child to have a Social Security number?

   _____

   _____

   _____

LESSON 7-6

FORM W-2

Everyone who earns more than a certain amount of money during a year must file a tax return. Filing means filling out the tax return forms and sending them to the Internal Revenue Service (IRS).

When you have worked for a business you will receive a Form W-2 from your employer. You must have a Form W-2 before you can complete your Federal Income Tax return. If you have not received a Form W-2 by January 31, or if it is incorrect, contact your employer. Form W-2 gives you the following information:

- How much money your employer paid you during the year

- How much money was taken out of your pay for Federal Income Tax

- How much money was taken out of your salary for Social Security (FICA)—Federal Insurance Contribution Act

If you need assistance in completing your tax form, you may obtain free help at your local IRS office. If there is no IRS office in your community, you can call the toll-free number listed in your telephone book under "U.S. Government, Treasury Department, Internal Revenue Service." Mail your tax return no later than April 15.

Below is a sample W-2 Form:

Form W-2 Wage and Tax Statement

1 Control number		
2 Employer's name, address, and ZIP code Budget Printing 2747 W. Lincoln St. Collins, TX 76034	3 Employer's identification number 000-00-0001 5 Statutory Deceased Legal 942 Subtotal Void employee ☒ ☐ rep ☐ emp ☐ ☐ 6 Allocated tips	4 Employer's State number 123456 7 Advance EIC payment
8 Employee's social security number 000-12-1982	9 Federal income tax withheld $154.00	10 Wages, tips, other compensation $3,250.00	11 Social security tax withheld $214.50
12 Employee's name, address, and ZIP code Kim Chang 500 E. Park St. Collins, TX 76034	13 Social security wages $3,250.00 16 Employer's use	14 Social security tips -0-
	17 State income tax $402.00	18 State wages, tips, etc. -0-	19 Name of State TX
	20 Local income tax -0-	21 Local wages, tips, etc. -0	22 Name of locality Collins Cty

1. Review the sample Form W-2 above. Use the information given to answer the following questions:

    (a) What is the employer's name? _____

    (b) What is the employee's name? _____

    (c) How much Social Security tax was withheld? _____

    (d) How much money did Kim make? _____

    (e) How much state income tax did Kim pay? _____

    (f) How much federal income tax was withheld? _____

    (g) What was the total amount of Kim's wages? _____

2. Kim also worked for a month at his church as a paid recreation leader. It is February 15, but he has not received Form W-2 from the church. What should he do?

    _____

    _____

3. Kim has found an error on his Form W-2. What should he do?

    _____

    _____

4. Kim has all of his Form W-2s and they are correct. What should he do next?

    _____

    _____

5. What is the deadline for filing a federal income tax return?

    _____

GLOSSARY

A

A.A. Alcoholics Anonymous. An organization that helps alcoholics and their families.

Abuser. A person who misuses drugs and mistreats his or her health.

Achieve. To accomplish or finish with success.

Achievement. Accomplishing something successfully by means of exertion, skill, practice, or perseverance.

Advertising. The act of attracting public attention to a product or service.

Aerobic exercise. Physical activity which speeds up breathing and heart rate.

Aerosol. A substance which consists of fine solid or liquid particles of gas that can be sprayed.

Alcoholic. A person suffering from compulsive drinking beyond the person's control.

Amphetamines. Drugs which stimulate the central nervous system.

Annual Percentage Rate (APR). An annual measure of the finance charge expressed as a percentage of the unpaid balance of a debt.

Anorexia nervosa. An extreme preoccupation with weight loss that endangers an individual's life and health.

Assets. The dollar amount of what an individual owns.

Atherosclerosis. A disease of the arteries.

B

Balance. The amount of money a person has in a checking or savings account.

Bank statement. The bank's monthly record of an individual's checking account.

Barter. To trade goods or services without the exchange of money.

Bronchitis. An inflammation of the bronchial tubes.

Bulimia. Periodic binge eating, alternating with intervals of dieting or self-starvation.

C

Calorie. A calorie is the amount of heat energy that will raise the temperature of a gram of water one degree centigrade.

Cancer. A malignant growth of tissue, usually ulcerating and tending to spread, causing ill health and death.

Carbon monoxide. A colorless, odorless, poisonous gas formed by the incomplete burning of carbon.

Carcinogens. Cancer-causing agents.

Cash Discount Act (1981). A law encouraging retailers to offer lower prices to customers who pay cash.

Certificate of deposit. A savings plan which requires a minimum deposit for a minimum of time.

Check register or check stub. The record of transactions in a checking account, including deposits and checks.

Chronic condition. A state that continues for a long time, as a chronic disease.

Cilia. Very small, hairlike projections found in the nasal cavity.

Cocaine. A crystalline alkaloid obtained from coca leaves.

Communication. The exchange of thoughts, messages, or ideas by speech, signals, or writing.

Compound interest. Interest that is computed on the sum of the principal plus the interest already earned.

Conflict. A struggle, clash, controversy, disagreement, or opposition between two or more persons.

Consumer. A buyer of goods or services.

Consumer Credit Protection Act (1969). A law stating that the consumer must be told the dollar amount and the annual percentage rate (APR) before credit is extended. It also limits a credit card holder's liability for unauthorized use to $50 per card.

Cosigner. An individual who signs a document jointly with another or others; i.e., cosigning a loan or mortgage.

Credit. The ability to buy something now and pay for it later.

D

Decision-making. The process of making conscious choices between two or more alternatives to achieve goals.

Default. To fail to pay a debt when it is due.

Demand. The willingness and ability of consumers to purchase goods and services at certain prices.

Dependence. The state of being influenced by something else.

Deposit. A written order directing the bank to add money to an account.

Deposit slip. A form used to deposit checks and cash into an account.

Depressants. Drugs which have a tranquilizing effect on the individual.

Discretionary time. Free time individuals can allocate any way they choose.

Downpayment. An initial payment at the time of purchase.

Drawer. The person who opens a checking account or writes a check. Also called a payor.

E

Economize. To use or manage with thrift.

Economy. The management of the resources of a country, community, or business, as in "the American economy."

Empathize. To be sensitive to another person's feelings, situation, and concerns.

Emphysema. A disease which affects the air sacs of the lungs causing breathing difficulties.

Environment. Everything that surrounds an organism or group of organisms.

Esteem. To regard with respect and admiration. To appreciate, as in the phrase, "He is highly esteemed."

Equal Credit Opportunity Act (1975, 1977). A law prohibiting discrimination against a credit applicant based on sex, marital status, religion, race, national origin, or receipt of public assistance.

F

Fair Credit Billing Act (1975). A law protecting a consumer's credit rating when there is a dispute about the amount owed on a credit card or revolving credit purchase. It gives consumers the opportunity to correct errors which may appear on their billing statements without damaging their credit rating.

Fair Credit Reporting Act (1971). A law assuring consumers fair treatment by credit-reporting agencies. It guarantees the individual's right to know the contents of his or her credit file.

Financial goals. The goals achieved through economic resources.

Fixed expenses. Regular, consistent expenses; i.e., school lunches.

Fraud. Deceptions deliberately practiced in order to secure unfair or unlawful gain.

G

Goal. An end or objective that is achieved through effort and planning.

Grass. A slang term for marijuana.

H

Habit. An action or behavior that has been learned and has become fixed by many repetitions.

Hallucinations. The perception of objects which do not exist or the experiencing of feelings which have no cause outside one's mind.

Heart disease. An abnormal condition of the heart or of the heart and circulatory system.

Homo sapiens. The taxonomic designation for modern man. A Latin term which translates as "a wise being." Human beings' ability to think distinguishes them from all other organisms.

I

"I" Messages. In communication, these are simple statements of fact about one's own feelings or thoughts.

Inflation. The general rise in the cost of goods and services.

Inhibition. An inner force, as a fear, that prevents the free expression of one's thoughts or desires.

Installment accounts. Charge accounts that require that consumers repay the amount owed in a specific number of payments over a certain amount of time.

Interest. In savings accounts, money paid by a financial institution to savers for the use of their money. In credit accounts, the cost of borrowing money included in the finance charge.

J

Judgment. The act of judging or making a decision.

L

Letter of application. A letter detailing an individual's interest in and qualifications for a specific job; it is sent to a potential employer.

Liabilities. The dollar value of what you owe.

Lung disease. An abnormal condition of the lungs or of the respiratory system.

M

Management. The process of using resources to achieve goals. Management is an art, a skill, and a method for improving the quality of human life.

N

Needs. The basic physical and emotional essentials which are necessary for survival or fulfillment.

Net worth. The dollar difference between an individual's assets and liabilities.

Nicotine. A poisonous substance found in small amounts in tobacco.

Non-discretionary time. Time that is regulated or scheduled by others.

Nutrients. Substances or ingredients which provide nourishment.

O

Open date. The stamped date on food products which indicates when the product should be sold to ensure freshness.

Optimize. To make the most effective use of.

Outstanding. (of checks and deposits) Not shown on a bank statement, but recorded on a checkbook stub.

Overdrawn. Having a check written in excess of the amount of money in a checking account.

P

Payee. The person to whom a check is written.

Peer pressure. The influence of people, usually of the same age group, with whom a person associates.

Pep pills. Stimulant types of medications, usually amphetamines.

Personality. The sum total of your emotional, social, physical, and mental characteristics. The word "personality" comes from the Latin word *persona*, which means person.

Physical fitness. Good physical condition; health; ability to function at one's best level.

Physiological. Of or pertaining to the body. Physiological needs are those necessary for survival: food, air, clothing, shelter.

Principal. The amount of money deposited by the saver.

Problem solving. Taking action to resolve a question or situation which is uncertain or difficult.

Procrastination. To put something off until another time; to postpone or delay needlessly.

R

Reconcile. To check the consistency between an individual's record of a checking account balance and the bank's statement.

Redress. To set right, remedy, rectify, correct, or adjust.

Regular or 30-day accounts. Charge accounts that require that a consumer pay the amount due in full each month.

Resourcefulness. The human capacity for effectively using the resources one has to cope with daily challenges.

Resources. All things and skills one uses to achieve a goal.

Respiratory system. The system of organs serving the functions of respiration, including the lungs and their nervous and circulatory pathways as well as the channels for continuous air exchange.

Responsibility. The things for which an individual is answerable or accountable; a duty, obligation, or burden.

Résumé. A summary of previous work experience, education, and other job qualifications.

Revolving or open-ended accounts. Charge accounts that permit the consumer to repay the debt monthly in full with no finance charge, or to make a partial payment each month, in which case there is a finance charge.

Right. A just claim legally, morally, or traditionally; i.e., the right to free speech.

Role. The expected social behavior of an individual.

S

Savings accounts. A plan offered by a financial institution that pays interest on the amount deposited.

Self-actualization. To reach one's potential.

Self-esteem. Respect for self or pride in oneself.

Service charge. A fee charged by a bank for services rendered.

Sniffing. Inhaling the fumes of certain substances to produce a sensation of mild intoxication.

Society. A group of human beings with common interests and beliefs.

Standards. Judgments used to measure progress towards goals. A synonym for standards is ideals.

Stimulants. Drugs (usually amphetamines) prescribed for fatigue and weight loss.

Suicide. The intentional killing of oneself.

Supply. The amount of something available to consumers.

Susceptible. Having little resistance.

T

Tar. Hundreds of types of chemicals which make up the majority of known carcinogens.

Time management. The conscious control of time to fulfill needs and achieve goals.

Tobacco. A tall annual plant covered with short sticky hairs having broad leaves and white or pink tube-shaped flowers. The product made from the dried leaves of this plant is used for smoking or chewing or as snuff.

U

Unit price. The cost of a product by weight or size.

Universal Product Code. A series of black marks found on product packages used by stores to maintain inventory and for pricing.

V

Values. Principles that guide behavior.

Variable expenses. Adjustable costs; inconsistent expenses depending on use—that is, the cost of gasoline and oil for an automobile.

W

Wellness. Keeping the body and mind well and fit through a balanced daily routine of diet, exercise, and good health habits.

Withdraw. To take money from an account.

Withdrawal slip. A form used to take money from an account.

Y

"You" Messages. In communication, these are statements that ascribe blame, are judgmental, and promote arguments.

INDEX

LIFE MANAGEMENT SKILLS

O'CONNOR • GOLDSMITH

HE13 SOUTH-WESTERN

THIS BOOK IS THE PROPERTY OF:

STATE _____ PROVINCE _____ COUNTY _____ PARISH _____ SCHOOL DISTRICT _____ OTHER _____	Book No. _____ Enter information in spaces to the left as instructed

ISSUED TO	Year Used	CONDITION	
		ISSUED	RETURNED
. . . .	. . . .		
. . . .	. . . .		
. . . .	. . . .		
. . . .	. . . .		
. . . .	. . . .		
. . . .	. . . .		
. . . .	. . . .		
. . . .	. . . .		

PUPILS to whom this textbook is issued must not write on any page or mark any part of it in any way, consumable textbooks excepted.

1. Teachers should see that the pupil's name is clearly written in ink in the spaces above in every book issued.
2. The following terms should be used in recording the condition of the book: New; Good; Fair; Poor; Bad.